Practical QlikView 2
Beyond Basic QlikView
By
Mark O'Donovan

CONTENTS

Copyright

Disclaimer

Title: Practical QlikView 2 - Beyond Basic QlikView

Version: 1.0

Introduction

"Knowledge isn't power until it is applied." – Dale Carnegie

This book is aimed at those of you who have at least 3-6 months experience of creating QlikView documents and would like to gain a better understanding of some of the more advanced aspects of QlikView development.

If you have already worked through the book 'Practical QlikView' you should be ready to tackle the topics covered in this book.

A brief overview of the different sections contained within this book :

Section 1: User Interface

This Section contains chapters relating to building the qlikview user interface.

Chapter 1 - QlikView Design
This chapter will cover various design tips and techniques that can be used when developing your qlikview documents.

For example how to keep your documents looking consistent, where is the best place to position sheet objects like logos and the current selections box.

Chapter 2 - Advanced Sheet Objects
In this chapter we will explore sheet objects in more detail especially the chart object.

We will cover various examples including how to create dynamic charts, custom chart formatting and creating links to documents from within your chart object.

We will conclude this chapter with a simple introduction to QlikView Extensions.

Chapter 3 - Create your own extension
In the final chapter of this section we will cover the various files used to create your own qlikview extension using one of the sample QlikView extensions as a starting point.

We will cover various options you can use when creating your qlikview extension.

Creating a qlikview extension can include topics such as css, jquery and javascript that are used in normal web development. We have included urls to useful websites where you can find further information about these topics at the end of the book.

Section 2: QlikView Data

Within QlikView the data model is king.

If you get your data model right then creating the rest of the document should be relatively straightforward.

Chapter 1 - Managing the QlikView Data Model
We cover the qlikview data model, using link tables to assist in creating a cleaner data model and various types of table joins we can use in the loadscript.

Chapter 2 - QVD - QlikView Data
This is a very important topic to become familiar with when developing qlikview documents. We will cover various aspects of qvd creation including incremental qvd loads and qvd optimization.

Chapter 4 - QVX - Custom Data sources
When developing qlikview documents there may come a time when you need to access data that is not in a simple spreadsheet, database or text file.

In this chapter we will cover how you can create your own QlikView data sources called qlikview connectors using QVX and Microsoft Visual Studio Express (Free version).

Chapter 4 - Set Analysis
In this chapter we look into set analysis in more detail including examples using date fields, wildcards and the P() function.

Chapter 5 - Scripting - Techniques and Functions
This chapter covers a variety of functions and techniques including alternate states, aggr and the class function.

Chapter 6 - Security – Section Access
This final chapter of the section covers various aspects of document level security.

For example, how to filter documents based on the user login and how to setup the security in the loadscript as well as how to store security settings in other data sources.

Appendices

Appendix A:QlikView Server - QlikView at Work
This appendix covers how to install and setup your qlikview server. This was not included in the main part of the book because it requires a QlikView Server license. Other topics covered include QlikView Server security, configurable ODBC and QlikView Workbench.

Appendix B: QlikView Server Tools
In this appendix we cover a couple of qlikview server tools that might prove useful.

Appendix C: Useful Websites
Finally a list of qlikview and non-qlikview websites you might find useful especially when working on the QlikView Extensions examples.

License Requirements

The examples covered here have been created using QlikView Personal Edition 11.2.

Where you require an extra license such as a QlikView server license to cover an example it will be highlighted. Because most users will not have access to such licenses unless they are working within a company that uses QlikView these examples have been placed in the appendix and are meant to demonstrate what QlikView can do if you start using it within a working environment.

Sample data and examples for use with this book can be downloaded from the following url:

http://practical-qlikview.com/Downloads.aspx

If you have any problems downloading the samples please email info@practical-qlikview.com for help or use the contact page http://practical-qlikview.com/Contact.aspx.

Section 1: QlikView User Interface

Improving the design and usability of dashboards such as QlikView documents

In my experience once you consistently use design rules in the development of your QlikView document you will find that not only will you be able to develop your QlikView documents faster but the users of your QlikView documents will be happier with your documents as they will know what to expect.

The truth of the matter is that users don't really like change. Most people can and do live with things that have been designed poorly. Part of what makes a well designed QlikView document is that users come to expect where certain elements should be such as the current selections list.

In this chapter I will describe the most important design techniques to keep in mind when creating your QlikView documents followed by some specific tips, useful tools and some examples of 'good' design.

Many of these techniques can equally be applied to other reporting software and are not unique to QlikView.

One thing to keep in mind is that good design can be quite subjective and everyone will have their own preferences. This is especially true when it comes to fonts and colours used in documents.

1. QlikView Design

Create consistency between sheets and documents

Design techniques all about creating consistency.

The ability to create consistency in your QlikView document and also between QlikView documents is extremely important.

Users do not like to figure out how to use a QlikView document because the same functions are presented differently in different documents.

Creating consistency between QlikView documents can be a challenge when there are multiple QlikView developers that each have their own preferences for the design of QlikView documents.

For example, Microsoft has a standard for developing their applications in order to create consistency between applications.

But when Microsoft changed the layout of their menu system to add the ribbon bar the change created some confusion to begin with because users found it difficult to find the same options that they used in the previous version of the application.

If you follow a set of rules when creating your QlikView documents you will find that consistency follows. How difficult it is to apply design rules will affect how long you spend on the design aspects of your QlikView development.

Creating templates the standard document layout and basic of design of objects as well as using themes can make the task of creating the initial design of QlikView documents easier.

User Interface consistency - For example keeping captions looking the same, consistent colours used.

Data model consistency – For example naming of fields especially key fields.

Give user friendly names to fields that will be used for selection in the user interface, the reason for this is that they name of the field in the data model is what will be displayed in the 'Current Selections' object.

Next are a list of techniques and options which we can use in QlikView to create consistency and also simplify the development process.

Keep the designs as simple as possible

1. Try not to confuse users with chart types they are not familiar with such as radar charts.

2. Think about Colours – Do you have colour bind users?

   On the QlikView design course I attended only 1 person was concerned with colour bind users and the selection of colours for those users.

   For colour blind users - use different shades of the same colour.

3. Use muted pastally colours, use bright colours to draw attention to something like an error.

Screen Layout

1. Top left corner - place the most important object - this is most normally the current selection list. If possible try to avoid putting logos in this position as they are just distracting to the user.

2. For example put selection lists, current selections and the search object down the left hand side of the sheet and calendar selections at the top of the sheet.

3. You can even try putting the logo in the bottom left can corner of the screen and reduce the height of the banner at the top of the screen.

LOGO

4. Give most space to most important information.
   For example try keeping charts of equal importance to the same size.

5. If the legends on the X axis are too long you might want to set the legend to a slant or changing the chart to a horizontal bar chart or using the staggered axis.

   This is done on the Axes tab of the Chart properties by selecting the 'Staggered Labels' checkbox as shown in the screenshot below:

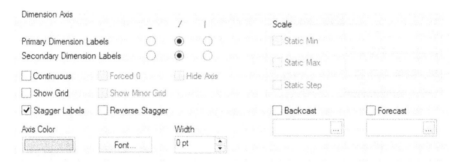

6. An example of a chart with Staggered labels is shown here, the main advantage is that labels are more readable:

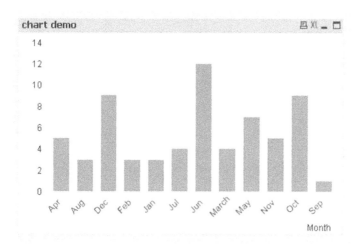

7. **Group objects**
   By using the same colour behind the objects or a border, for example creating coloured rectangle using a text object on the left hand side of the screen for selection list boxes.

8. **Put the detail on another sheet**
   Have selections and overviews of the data on one sheet with the detail level on a separate sheet. This can be a useful technique to prevent pivot tables becoming too large. Less memory will be used by the document when the sheet is not selected.

   The performance of the qlikview document can also be improved by forcing the user to make selections before for example a pivot table that is uses fields from a very large table of data is displayed. These considerations are more important when the QlikView document is used with large amounts of data and multiple users.

9. **Remove unnecessary elements**
   The might see obvious but is sometimes overlooked in an effort to try give the end user everything they might require.

Object Design

1. **Create an object design sheet**
   An object design sheet would consist of all the objects such as charts and tables setup with the default style such as colours and fonts.

2. You then copy and paste these objects when creating new documents to maintain consistency between sheets and documents.
   You can see an example of such as design sheet in the QlikView Developer Toolkit that comes with the QlikView desktop :

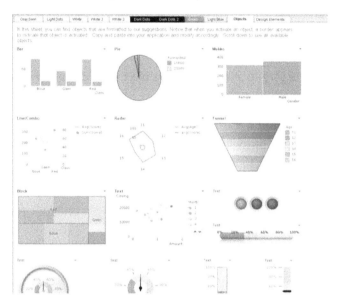

   To get started have a look at the QlikView Developer Toolkit which can be accessed from the Start Page when you first open QlikVIew, then select 'Getting Started, scroll down and click on the 'QlikView Developer Toolkit icon.

3. Reuse ideas from the demos on the QlikView website http://eu.demo.qlikview.com.

4. Set charts to predefined sizes.

Script Library

5. **Create a library of useful scripts.**.For example:

   o   Scripts to implement incremental qvds.

   o   Create a master calendar table to have common selections of dates for each sheet.

Sheet Templates

1. Create a template sheet with the main objects such as current selection, search object and logo that will be on every sheet.

   Then when creating a new sheet press CTRL+A , CTRL+C to copy all the documents from the template sheet and right click on the new sheet and select 'Paste Sheet Object as Link', this will create linked objects.

2. If you change the location of a linked object you can right click on the object, select Linked Objects, then 'Adjust Position of Linked Objects.

   This will have the effect of updating the position of all the other linked objects.

3. Keep the banner at the top of the screen as small as possible to avoid wasted space at banner 60px high might be all you really need.

4. All objects should have the same caption colour except the Current Selections box. This will mean that the current selections box will stand out more than the other objects.

5. Choose theme of colours to use 3/4 colours and no other - check company website ie: use corporate colours for caption bar - chart bars matching caption bar colour. Obviously this might not work well if the corporate colours are bright red and green.

6. Use off white background – not so bright and less tiring on the eyes if using the QlikView document for long periods of time.

7. Selection \ search left side of screen (or top right under dates).

8. Use sans serif fonts – such arial\ verdana \ tahoma\ Calibri.

9. Use same colour behind group of objects. For example to group selection objects.

10. When designing the layout of your document in QlikView know what size of screen you are developing for and resize the window using the View-Resize Window option.

    By remembering to resize the window you will avoid unnecessary horizontal\vertical scrolling.

Chart Types

Bar Charts

The most common chart type is the bar chart.

Use a single colour for the bar colour as using multi-coloured bars does not normally add anything useful.

Line Charts

Line charts are used to represent values that are changing over time for example time , date or some period of time.

For example think of computer performance data where the amount of memory used is plotted over time in the Windows Task Manager or the profits of a company might be plotted over time to see how well the company is performing.

Pie Charts\Funnel Charts

The problem with pie \ funnel chart types is that it is difficult to compare areas effectively.

If possible instead of a pie chart you could use a bar chart.

Funnel charts are commonly used for sales pipelines but can cause problems if you need to compare more than 1 funnel chart.

Useful Design Tools

For finding out which colors that go together:

http://www.colorschemer.com/colorpix_info.php

http://jiminy.medialab.sciences-po.fr/tools/palettes

https://kuler.adobe.com

An Open Source vector graphics editor – very useful for creating images:

http://inkscape.org/

Looking for different fonts:

http://www.fontsquirrel.com/

Summary

Think about the users - talk to users

Think of the end users – current and future users (and developers) - Add welcome sheet to describe the documents tabs.

Remember to add help text to objects where descriptions would be useful.
The help text field is in the properties caption tab of objects.

If possible see how the users use your QlikView documents. re: log files.

If you are using the QlikView Server you can setup audit logs in the QlikVIew Management console to discover the objects that users are actually using.

Talk to your marketing department

If you are developing QlikView documents within a company it may prove useful to talk to people in the marketing department especially the designers to find out what design guidelines the following when creating marketing documents for the company.

Also, if you can talk to web designers within the company they may be able to advise you on any company preferences for things such as fonts. So that you can create the same look and feel in your QlikView document as in other websites.

The aim of this chapter on design was to give you a few tips to aid when developing QlikView documents from a design perspective.

If you would like to look into design in more depth I would suggest starting with the following book by Stephen Few:

Information Dashboard Design: The Effective Visual Communication of Data by Stephen Few

Personally I find having a set of techniques that I can remember and are therefore more likely to use more useful.

Whereas reading books that are focused on the design of dashboards will certainly an insight into questions such as why you don't see that many radar charts on QlikView documents. But you might not remember all the design tips months after reading them.

My advice is to start using a few techniques on a regular basis until they become second nature and progress from there.

2. Advanced Sheet Objects

In this section we will be covering the more advanced and arguably more interesting aspects of the chart object.

When developing QlikView documents most people focus on the Bar Chart and basic pivot\straight tables as they are the most popular chart types.

In this chapter we will cover how to:

- Create http links in fields so that you can link to images\documents such as pdf files.

- Add trendlines to your charts, for example to display the average of some expression.

- Create sparklines and other mini charts.

Data for Chart Examples

This is the data that will be used for the chart examples.

1. Open the SampleCustomerReports.xls spreadsheet and read the "source data" sheet in using a loadscript such as the one below:

```
LOAD Product,
    Customer,
    [Qtr 1],
    [Qtr 2],
    [Qtr 3],
    [Qtr 4]
FROM
[SampleCustomerReports.xls]
(biff, embedded labels, table is [Source Data$]);
```

2. Reload your document.

    When using the Chart Object you need to select the right chart type we will cover some of the other chart types that are available to use within the chart object and any pitfalls to keep in mind when using them.

Guages

Guage chart types are used to plot single values against ranges, when you think of gauges think of a speedometer in a car where the current speed of the car is displayed against the minimum and maximum possible speeds.

Another example is:

Total Sales for the month might be plotted against:

Poor Sales   1-10m

Average Sales   11-20m

Excellent Sales 21-100m

Guage Example

1. Make sure the data is loaded into a new qlikview document, if not see the section 'Data for Chart Examples' at the start of this chapter.

2. Create a chart object:

3. Set the chart type to Guage (General tab).

4. Set the Expression to =sum([Qtr 1])

5. Presentation tab:

    a. The definition of the segments of the guage are set in the Presentation tab.

    b. Make the following changes:

        i. Uncheck the 'Autowidth segments' - when this option is selected each segment has an equal area of the guage.

        ii. Set the Max value in the Guage Settings to 200000 (the total of the expression sum([Qtr 1]) should be 138288.9.

        iii. Segment setup: The lower bound for each setup defines the value at which the segment starts.

        iv. Add another segment , select each segment and set the label, lower bound and colour as follows:

	Segment 1	Segment 2	Segment 3
Label	Poor	Average	Excellent
Lower Bound	0.0	100000	150000
Colour	Red	Orange	Green

6. Click on OK and the result should look like the image below:

Funnels

Sales people seem to love Funnel charts to display their sales pipeline.

Business Intelligence developers seem to have fixed views on them but tend to add them to dashboards because that is what the end user expects to see.

In this example will use the funnel chart to display the total of sales in each quarter.

Funnel example

1. Create a chart object using the same data as in the Guage example.

2. Create 4 expressions to calculate the total of each quater:

=sum([Qtr 1])

=sum([Qtr 2])

=sum([Qtr 3])

=sum([Qtr 4])

3. On the presentation tab you will see that the default 'Data Proportionality' option is:

    'Segment Height Proportional to Data'

4. Click OK and you will see that your funnel chart will look like the screenshot below:

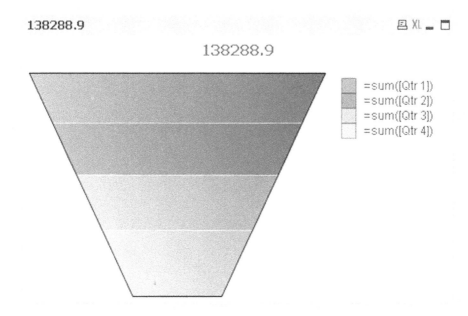

5. Go back to the chart properties, presentation tab and now select Segment Area Proportional to Data and your chart should now look like the following screenshot:

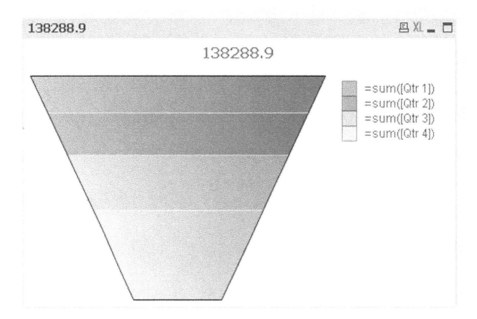

I think most problems with funnels occur when you select the Equal Segment Heights option as there is no real value added by the chart.

Also these charts are not suitable when it comes to comparing segments in 2 different funnel charts for example if you wanted to compare the quarterly totals for 2 different years, in these cases it is probably best to use a bar chart.

Line chart

Line charts are commonly used to represent values that are changing over time for example time , date or some period of time.

In this example we are going plot the sales total for one particular company over the 4 quarters.

Line chart example

1. First we need to change the loadscript to use the crosstable feature as shown in the script below:

```
CrossTable(Quarter, Amount, 2)
LOAD Product,
    Customer,
    [Qtr 1],
    [Qtr 2],
    [Qtr 3],
    [Qtr 4]
FROM
SampleCustomerReports.xls
(biff, embedded labels, table is [Source Data$]);
```

2. The cross table option:

   Crosstable(attribute,data, no qualifier fields)

   Attribute field - in this case it is Quarter and will be Qtr1-4.

   Data - this is set to Amount and is the sales figure.

   No Qualifier fields - This is the number of fields to ignore before the Attribute\Data fields. In this case it is the 2 fields Product and Customer.

Product	Customer	Quarter	Amount
Alice Mutton	ANTON	Qtr 2	702
Alice Mutton	BERGS	Qtr 1	312
Alice Mutton	BOLID	Qtr 4	1170
Alice Mutton	BOTTM	Qtr 1	1170
Alice Mutton	ERNSH	Qtr 1	1123.2
Alice Mutton	ERNSH	Qtr 4	2607.15
Alice Mutton	GODOS	Qtr 2	280.8
Alice Mutton	HUNGC	Qtr 1	62.4
Alice Mutton	PICCO	Qtr 2	1560
Alice Mutton	PICCO	Qtr 3	936
Alice Mutton	RATTC	Qtr 2	592.8
Alice Mutton	REGGC	Qtr 4	741
Alice Mutton	SAVEA	Qtr 3	3900
Alice Mutton	SAVEA	Qtr 4	789.75
Alice Mutton	SEVES	Qtr 2	877.5
Alice Mutton	WHITC	Qtr 4	780
Aniseed Syrup	ALFKI	Qtr 4	60
Aniseed Syrup	BOTTM	Qtr 4	200

3. Once the document is reloaded the current table should have the four fields:

    Product
    Customer
    Quarter
    Amount

4. Create a new chart object and set the following options:

    General tab - Line chart

    Dimensions - select Quarter

    Expressions - =sum({<Customer={'BERGS'}>}[Amount])

    This expression is used to calculate the total sales amount for the customer BERGS.

5. Click OK and your line chart should look like the following screenshot:

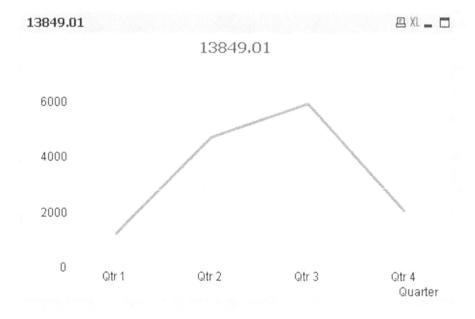

The advantage of using line charts instead of bar charts when plotting data over time is that it is easy to see trends especially when you have multiple values plotted on the same chart.

For example if we add the Dimension of Customer and change the expression used to include all customers that start with B:

=sum({<Customer={'B*'}>}[Amount])

Now multiple customers will be displayed, it is easy to see that Customer BERGS is doing very well until it comes to Qtr 4.

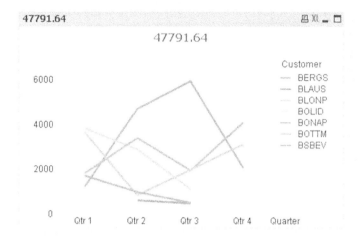

Where as if we now change this chart to a bar chart using the Chart type option in the General tab the chart will look like the next screenshot.

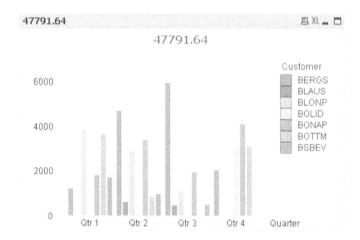

In this example it is not as easy to see the trends in the sales amounts for the customers between customers as in the line chart.

Dynamic charts

There are 2 ways you can create dynamic charts in QlikView. One way is to use 'Fast Change Type' in the General tab of the chart properties.

The other way that we will cover next is to setup dynamic dimensions and expressions in the loadscript. This can be a very useful technique to implement to save on space on your sheet and allow users to select which type of chart they wish to view especially when there are many potential charts different users require.

1. Using the same loadscript for the data as in the line chart example which is:

   ```
   CrossTable(Quarter, Amount, 2)
   LOAD Product,
       Customer,
       [Qtr 1],
       [Qtr 2],
       [Qtr 3],
       [Qtr 4]
   FROM
   SampleCustomerReports.xls
   (biff, embedded labels, table is [Source Data$]);
   ```

2. Add the following inline table.

   ```
   dynamic_charts:
   LOAD * INLINE [
       "Graph Name", Dimension1, Dimension2, Expression
       "Sales Amount by Quarter", Quarter, Customer, "=sum(Amount)"
       "B Customers - Sales Amount by Quarter", Quarter, Customer,
   "=sum({<Customer={'B*'}>}Amount)"
       ];
   ```

   This table will be used to change the dimensions, expression of the chart.

3. Create a new bar chart and make the following changes:

   a. General tab:

      Check the 'Show title in Char' option and set the text to:

      =[Graph Name]

      Select the Chart Type of Bar chart.

   b. Dimensions

4. Add the 2 calculated dimensions to use the dimension1 and dimension2 fields in the inline table setup in the loadscript:

   =$(=Dimension1)
   =$(=Dimension2)

5. Expressions -Add the following expression:

   $(=Expression)

6. Caption - Uncheck the option 'Show Caption'.

7. Click OK to display the chart.

8. Right click on the sheet and in the Fields tab add the field 'Graph Name' to the fields to be displayed in listboxes. Select an option in the Graph Name listbox, it will change the dimensions and expressions in the chart as you can see from the following 2 screenshots:

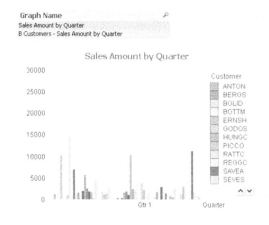

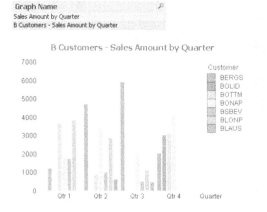

Trend lines

Trend lines can be used in scatter charts, line charts and in bar/combo charts where there is 1 dimension and 1 expression shown as bar.

1. Using the loadscript for the data as follows :

   ```
   customer_data:
    LOAD Product,
       Customer,
       [Qtr 1],
       [Qtr 2],
       [Qtr 3],
       [Qtr 4]
   FROM
   [SampleCustomerReports .xls]
   (biff, embedded labels, table is [Source Data$]);
   ```

2. Create a bar chart with the following settings:

3. Chart Type - Bar chart

4. Dimension - Customer

5. Dimension Limits - Show Only - Largest 5 Values and uncheck 'Show Others'.

6. Expressions - =sum([Qtr 1])

7. You should now have a chart looking like the screenshot below:

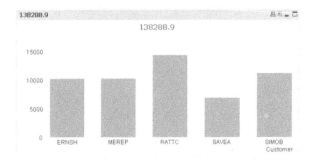

8. Go back to the Expressions tab of the chart properties to the Trendlines options.

9. Check the 'Average' Trendlines option as shown:

Trendlines

☑ Average   ☐ Show Equation
☐ Linear   ☐ Show R²
☐ Polynomial of 2nd c

10. Your chart should now show a line across the chart to denote in this example the Average sales in Qtr 1 across all customers.

In this example you can see the benefit of trendlines is that you can see which customers are performing above average (customer RATTC) as well as the customers performing below average (customer SAVEA) very easily.

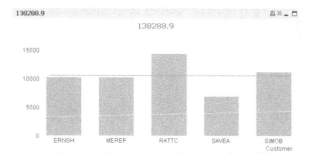

Linear trendline

A linear regression line which tries to find the best fitting line through the data. Regression lines can be used to try predict future values, for example a company might want to understand how the amount of money spent on marketing affected sales.

When using linear regression lines to predict it is assumed that the variables being plotted have a correlation.

1. Using the chart from the inital trendline example, select the trendline option 'Linear'.

2. Change the sort order of the customer dimension in the 'Sort tab' of the chart properties to 'Y-value' descending. Your trendline will now look like the next screenshot:

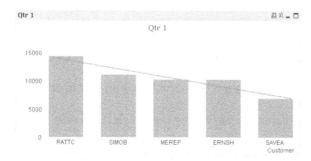

Sparklines and other mini charts

Sparklines are useful for showing trends especially where space is limited.

To use mini charts you must select a Chart Type of 'Straight table'.

1. Create another Chart table with a Dimension of Customer and 2 expressions of:

    =sum([Qtr 1])

2. Set the label of 1 expression to be 'Qtr 1' and the expression for the mini chart to 'Qtr1 Sales by Product'.

3. Within the Expressions tab of the straight table properties select 'Mini Chart' from the Representation dropdownlist for one of the expressions you created.

4. Click on the 'Mini Chart Settings' button and the following dialog box will appear:

Useful options include being able to make the Max\Min value with a different colour.

As you can see from the previous screenshot these are set to be Blue and Red by default.

5. Change the Dimension of the mini chart to be 'Product' and select a mode of sparkline, this will create the following table:

Qtr 1			
Customer	Qtr 1	Qtr1 Sales by Product	
	138288.9		
SAVEA	6942.63		
ERNSH	10259.71		
MEREP	10272.56		
SIMOB	11183.4		
RATTC	14364.2		

6. In this example we can see if there is a large difference between the amount of sales by each of the top 5 performing customers for Quarter 1 (Qtr 1).

Although the sparkline is a popular choice you can experiment with other mini chart types using the 'Mode' drop downlist including dots,lines with dots,bars and whiskers.

Custom Chart Formatting

A common request from users is to set the colour of cells in a chart based on another expression, for example to highlight invoices not paid, salesmen not hitting targets or a threshold being exceeded.

Custom Chart Formatting example:

1. Add the follow loadscript to a new QlikView document and reload the document.
   user_details:
   LOAD * INLINE [
       Name, Amount
       UserA, 10
       UserB, 20
       UserC, 30
   ];

2. Create the following chart with the Name as the dimension and =sum(Amount) as the expression.

60	凰 Xl _ ▢
Name	=sum(Amount)
	60
UserA	10
UserB	20
UserC	30

Dimensionality() function

The Dimensionality function is useful when you wish to apply an expression depending on the aggregation level. For example, you wish to change the background colour for rows that have an Amount field of greater or equal to 15.

1. If we made the following changes in the visual cues tab of the chart properties:

2. You will see that the background colour of the total field has also been changed as well as the row values that are greater equal\greater than 15.

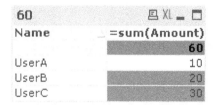

3. To avoid changing the background of the total field , in the Expressions tab expand the settings, select 'Background Color' :

4. Right click on the 'Background Color' options and select Edit expression and add the following expression:

=if(Dimensionality()=1 and sum(Amount)>=15,RGB(255,0,0))

   a. The Dimensionality value of the total field is 0.

   b. If the result of dimensionality() is 1 , ie: not the total field in this case and the sum(Amount) is greater\equal to 15 then set the background colour using the RGB function, the result is shown in the next screenshot.

Linking to images and other documents

Creating links to other documents from within QlikView documents can make the QlikView document even more useful with very little effort.

For example a home user might create links to their personal photos whereas a user for a company might create links to pdf documents or invoices or digital signatures.

Link Example

In this example we will create a simple inline table to link to a text file.

1. Create a folder called c:\myfiles, within this folder create a couple of text files in c:\ called test1.txt and test2.txt.

2. Add some text to each file so that you know it is the correct file when you click on the link to open it.

3. Create a new QlikView document and edit the loadscript to add the following inline table:

```
link_example:
LOAD * INLINE [
    name, path
    test file one, c:\myfiles\test1.txt
    test file two, c:\myfiles\test2.txt
];
```

4. This simple inline table will provide the name and path to files which we shall use in the chart object.

5. Reload your document.

6. Create a new chart object with the following settings:

    a. General: Chart type - Straight table.

    b. Dimensions: Used Dimensions - name.

    c. Expressions: Definition

        The format of the link expressions is :

        <Text for the link> & '<url>' & <path_to_attachment>

        In this example use the following expression:

=name & '<url>' & path

Label - 'Link'

   d.   Display options

       In this example the 'Representation' field has to be set to 'Link'.

7. The definition of the Link field has to include the text '<url>' which separates the text that will be displayed in the table from the url of the link.

8. If the 'Representation' field has to be set to 'Image' and the field definition is the name of a field with the path to the image, then the image will be displayed in the table.

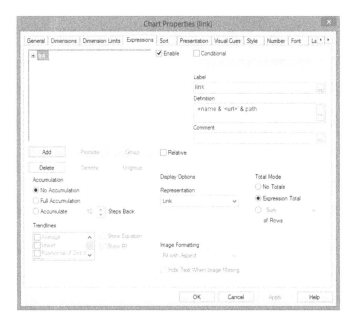

9. Make sure the following option is set:
Settings -> User Preferences -> Design -> Always Show Design Menu Items

10. Right click on cell -> Custom Format Cell -> blue text colour and underlined. This will mean that the link will look like a normal http link.

11. Your chart object with the links should now look like the following screenshot :

12. Click on the links to confirm that they open the documents correctly.

Simple Extension example

1. Before getting started with extensions you will need to install the extensions on your machine.

2. Open C:\Program Files\QlikView\Examples\Extensions in Windows Explorer.

3. Double click on the file Extension Examples.qar (qar is for QlikView Archive).

4. If the extensions are installed you will see a dialog box similar the next screenshot:

5. Close and reopen the QlikView Desktop Application.

6. To get an example of what extensions can add to your QlikView document go to the 'Getting Started' page and select the 'Extensions Examples' document.

7. If you do not see the extensions in this document that the webview is turn on in the View->Turn on/off webview option.

8. Once you can see the extensions in the 'Extension examples' document you can then start using the extensions yourself.

Web Page Viewer Extension

The webpage extension is one of the simplest extensions, this extension displays a webpage within your QlikView document.
This webpage can be based on a static URL or on a URL from an expression.

One practical purpose of the webpage extension would be to display a webpage within your QlikView document so that the user did not have to navigate away from your QlikView document for example you could display the company intranet or google for searching,

In the next example we will show a simple example of how you can use the webpage extension.

1. Open QlikView and create a new document.

2. Set the WebView on using the option from the view menu.

3. Right click on the sheet and select 'new sheet object'.

4. Select the extension objects option, drag and drop the webpage viewer to your sheet.

5. You will see that the default web page is the QlikView.com website as shown below:

6. Next, we will alter the webpage viewer object to display a different website. Right click on the webpage viewer object and select the properties option.

7. Select the webpage viewer option and enter the URL for a new website. In this example we have entered the URL for the practical-qlikview.com website.

8. Once you have entered the website of your choice right click on the properties dialogue box and select close to see the website displayed.

Summary

In this chapter we covered some if the different chart type available and some useful techniques such as creating custom formatting and creating links to files within the chart.

Next we will cover how you create your own sheet objects in the webview (not using the IE plugin) using qlikview extensions.

3. Create your own extension

Extensions can add some great features to your QlikView document.

For example you can display calendars, other web pages and integrate your qlikview document with google maps.

There are 2 different types of extensions:

Object extensions

1. Allow you to create a custom object that you can add to your qlikview document.

2. For example, displaying a webpage within the qlikview document.

Document extensions

3. Allow you to add functionality that can affect the entire qlikview document.

4. Enable document extensions in the Settings->Document Properties-Extensions tab.

5. For example, setting a qlikview variable to identify what type of browser is being used.

In this example we are going to show how you can make your own custom QlikView extension.

To do this we will modify an existing simple extension and explain the various files go to make up the extension.

When you have completed this example, you will have the knowledge to start creating your own extensions and making the effort is definitely worthwhile as the ajax web client is becoming more and more important in QlikView development especially in environments were mobile devices such as Ipads and browsers other than internet explorer need to access your QlikView documents.

Although the complexity of your extension will depend to some degree on your knowledge of other languages such as JavaScript.

For a good introduction to Javascript visit http://w3schools.com.

The location of the QlikView extensions is:

%UserProfile%\AppData\Local\QlikTech\QlikView\Extensions\Objects

Using the webpage viewer extension as an example we will cover the main files that make up an object extension.

The files that go to make up an extension are as follows:

Definition.xml

The definition.xml file defines the fields that will be used in the properties dialogue box.

Dynproperties.qvpp & Properties.qvpp

These qvpp files define the properties dialogue box which is displayed when you right click on the extension object.

Icon.png

The icon file is displayed in the 'Select new object' menu option when you right click on the sheet in the web view within QlikView.

Script.js

The script.js file contains the JavaScript that will be used to provide the functionality of the extension.

To being with it is probably best to start with examples that are near to the solution your require and modify them for your particular needs. This will aid learning as you will have less to focus on and mean that you can start creating useful solutions faster.

For a good introduction to Javascript visit http://w3schools.com.

For more useful links see appendix C.

Extension example

1. First copy the webpageviewer folder so that you have a backup before you start editing the files.

2. Location of WebPageViewer Extension:

%UserProfile%\AppData\Local\QlikTech\QlikView\Extensions\Objects\QlikView\Examples\WebPageViewer

For example:

C:\Users\myprofilename\AppData\Local\QlikTech\QlikView\Extensions\Objects\QlikView\Examples\WebPageViewer

3. You can think of an extension object as a chart object. In fact if you go the the Settings -> Sheet Properties option and then selection the Objects tab you will see that the Object Type for the extension you have created is 'Bar Chart'.

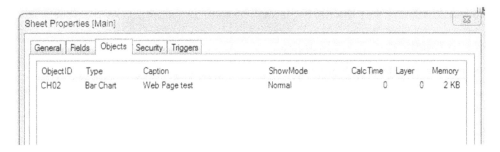

This will make more sense when we cover creating dimensions and measures for the extension.

4. Next we will cover how the webpageviewer files and various ways that you can customized these files and they affect changes have on the qlikview extension object.

Definition.xml

The definition.xml file defines the fields that will be used in the properties dialogue box. Below is the example of the definition of definition.xml file used for the web page viewer extension:

```
<?xml version="1.0" encoding="utf-8"?>
<ExtensionObject Label="Web Page Viewer" Description="Web page in a
frame">
    <Initiate Name="Chart.BgColor.ColorHex" value="#E0FFE0" />
    <Text Label="Url" Initial=""
Expression="='http://www.qlikview.com/'"/>
    <Initiate Name="Caption.Text" value="Web Page" />
</ExtensionObject>
```

Next we will cover the various options that can be used in the definition.xml file.

ExtensionObject

As you can see from the previous example of a definition.xml file the ExtensionObject is the main tag.

Type = this attribute can be set to either object or document, default is object.

PageWidth = default = 20

PageHeight = default = 40

The Label, Name and Description options are displayed when you hover over the Extension Object in the 'New Sheet Object' options.

Text Options

General text options

Label - the text on the left hand side of the text field.

Width ie: Width="100%" or Width="100px"

Expression
You can use the expression option to set default values for the field for example:

This will set the color picker to default to light blue:

<Text Label="Color1" Type="color" Initial="" Expression="#80FFFF"/>

Whereas this will set the default webpage for this field:

<Text Label="Url" Initial="" Expression="='http://www.qlikview.com/'"/>

Type
The Type option defines the type of field that is added to the properties page.
Text is the default type, for example this is a textfield with label or Url and field set to the qlikview.com url:

<Text Label="Url" Initial="" Expression="='http://www.qlikview.com/'"/>

Other Type Options
NOTE: The Type options are case sensitive so if you use Type="Color" instead of Type="color" it will default to a textbox.

Checkbox

<Text Label="Checkbox example" Type="checkbox" Initial="" Expression="1"/>

Color

This option provides the user with a useful color picker:

1. Add the following line within the ExtensionObject tags in the definiton.xml file and save the file:

   <Text Label="Color:" Type="color" Initial="" />

2. Press F5 to refresh the page.

3. Right click on the web page extension object you created and select properties.

4. You will now see a color picker has been added like the one shown in the screenshot below:

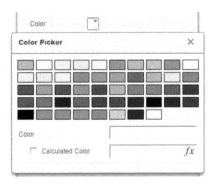

Select - HTML Dropdownlist

1. Add the following code to the Definition.xml file under the last Text option.

<Text Label="Options:" Type="select" select="noselection,one,two,three" Selectlabel="Make a selection"/>

2. The first option is the select comma separated list is the value that is used when no selection is made. For example:

```
<?xml version="1.0" encoding="utf-8"?>
<ExtensionObject Label="My website" Description="Display my website">
        <Initiate Name="Chart.BgColor.ColorHex" value="#E0FFE0" />
        <Text Label="Url" Initial=""
Expression="='http://www.qlikview.com/'"/>
        <Text Label="Checkbox example" Type="checkbox" Initial="checked"
Expression="1"/>
        <Text Label="Options:" Type="select"
select="noselection,one,two,three" Selectlabel="Make a selection"/>
        <Initiate Name="Caption.Text" value="Web Page from def" />
</ExtensionObject>
```

3. Press F5 to refresh the page, you will then see that the DynProperties.qvpp file has updated with the following code:

```
<select style='width:94%;' avq='mySelect:.Chart.Text.2.Content'>

        <option value='noselection'>Make a selection</option>
        <option value='one'>one</option>
        <option value='two'>two</option>
        <option value='three'>three</option>
</select>
```

4. Final version of the defintion.xml showing all the Type options:

```
<?xml version="1.0" encoding="utf-8"?>
<ExtensionObject Label="My website" Description="Display my website">
    <Initiate Name="Chart.BgColor.ColorHex" value="#E0FFE0" />
    <Text Label="Url" Initial=""
Expression="='http://www.qlikview.com/'"/>
    <Text Label="Checkbox example" Type="checkbox" Initial="checked"
Expression="1"/>
    <Text Label="Options:" Type="select"
select="noselection,one,two,three" Selectlabel="Make a selection"/>
    <Text Label="Color:"  Type="color" Initial="" />
    <Initiate Name="Caption.Text" value="Web Page from def" />
</ExtensionObject>
```

Dimensions

As previously mentioned extension objects can be thought of as chart objects in the qlikview document. Below we show how to define 2 dimensions used in the extension.

```
<Dimension Label="My Dimension 1" Initial="" TargetName="test dim1" />
<Dimension Label="My Dimension 2" Initial="" TargetName="test dim2" />
```

Measurement

Measurements are the equivalent of expressions in your chart. The example below creates 1 measurement called "My Measure1" with no inital value.

    <Measurement Label="My Measure 1" Initial=""/>

PropertiesPage

    <PropertiesPage [Version="11"] [File=""] />

This option will enable you to have a special properties.qvpp for Qlikview version 11, for example: <PropertiesPage Version="11" File="Properties.qvpp" />

Initiate

Used to initalize QlikView properties.
In this example the line below is setting the Caption text.

    <Initiate Name="Caption.Text" value="Web Page" />

Set the first dimension:

    <Initiate Name="Chart.Dimension.0.Field" Value="MyField" />

Qvpp files : Dynproperties.qvpp

QlikView 11 can create property pages dynamically once you selected 'New Sheet Object'.

If you delete the current DynProperties.qvpp file you might need to close and reopen the document for a new DynProperties.qvpp file to be recreated.

These qvpp files define the properties dialogue box which is displayed when you right click on the extension object as shown in the screenshot below:

These files are overwritten by settings from the definiton.xml file.For example if you change the line in the definiton.xml file:

<ExtensionObject Label="Web Page Viewer" Description="Web page in a frame">

to

<ExtensionObject Label="My website" Description="Display my website">

Then press F5 to refresh the extension you will see that when you right click on the web page object and select properties that the section has been updated as shown below:

Open the Dynproperties.qvpp file you will see that the label has been updated from 'Web Page Viewer' to 'My website' .

For this reason you should make sure that you update fields in the definition.xml file otherwise your changes will be overwritten when you reopen the document. For example:

```
<div class="ToolWindow-MainBody" avq="foldOutMenu:." style="overflow:
visible !important; float: left;">
```

```
<div class="prop-accordion" avq="accordion:.">
    <h3 class="prop-h3 accordion-shadow">
        <a href="#">My website</a>
    </h3>
    <div class="prop-grid_container accordion-shadow-enabler"
style="overflow:auto;">
```

Rename the Dynproperties.qvpp files to Properties.qvpp and add the following line to the definition.xml file, this will allow you to modify the qvpp file:

<PropertiesPage Version="11" File="Properties.qvpp" />

AVQ

To connect the fields in the qvpp properties file to data you need to add an avq (or 'avqcol' attribute) to the elements in the file:

The basic format of the avq attribute is :

avq=verb[:property]

Or

avqcol=verb[:property][:extra]

Verb

The type of command for example prop_checkbox to create a checkbox.

Property

Set the property to which the element is connected, for example:

<div class='prop-grid_span-7' avq='prop_dynamicDropdown:.Chart.Dimension.0.Field'></div>

The property is Chart.Dimension.0.Field, which means that the element is bound to the first dimension of the chart.

Some examples of possible verbs are listed below:

prop_label

This is used for labels for example:

```
<div class='prop-grid_clear prop-grid_prepend-1 prop-grid_span-5' avq='prop_label'>My
Dimension 1</div>
```

prop_dynamicDropdown

Creates a drop down listbox for dimensions, for example:

```
<div class='prop-grid_span-7' avq='prop_dynamicDropdown:.Chart.Dimension.0.Field'></div>
```

prop_editexpression

Create a textbox for with an edit expression dialog, for example:

```
<div class='prop-grid_span-7 prop-grid_last' style='width:94%;'
avq='prop_editexpression:.Chart.Expression.0.0.Definition'></div>
```

prop_checkbox

Create a checkbox, for example:

```
<div class='prop-grid_clear prop-grid_span-1'
avq='prop_checkbox:.Chart.Text.1.Content'></div>
```

mySelect

Create a HTML dropdownlist, for example:

```
<select style='width:94%;' avq='mySelect:.Chart.Text.2.Content'>

    <option value='noselection'>Make a selection</option>
    <option value='one'>one</option>
    <option value='two'>two</option>
    <option value='three'>three</option>
</select>
```

prop_dlgbuttonjqui

Create a button that opens a dialog, for example:

```
<div class='prop-width-28px' propicontype='tool'

avq='prop_dlgbuttonjqui:.Chart.Dimension.0:ExtensionDimDialog.qvpp'>
</div>
```

panels

Include another qvpp file, for example, this example creates another panel using the layout in the file layout.qvpp:

```
<div class="prop-grid_container accordion-shadow-enabler"
avq="panel::Layout.qvpp"></div>
```

Reference first text field

This example creates an input textfield for the first text field references as follows :
`Chart.Text.0.Content.`

```
<td class="ToolProperty-Literal">
    Label1
</td>
<input style="width: 200px" avq="edit:.Chart.Text.0.Content" />
avq="panel::Layout.qvpp"
 <tr class="ToolProperty-Header" ><td>Layout</td><th></th></tr>
```

Icon.png

The icon file is displayed in the 'New Sheet Object' menu option when you right click on the sheet in the web view within QlikView.

Custom Extension Full Example

Below is the full code used to demonstrate the extension options. For code for this example is available from the download page on practical-qlikview.com.

Although it is useful to see the actual code here you will benefit from downloading the samples code and experimenting by making simple changes and trying out the examples presented in this chapter.

Definition.xml

```xml
<?xml version="1.0" encoding="utf-8"?>

<ExtensionObject Label="My website" Description="Display my website">
    <Dimension Label="My Dimension 1" Initial="" TargetName="test dim1"
/>
    <Measurement Label="Measure" Initial=""/>
    <Text Label="Url" Initial=""
Expression="='http://www.qlikview.com/'"/>
    <Text Label="Checkbox example" Type="checkbox" Initial=""
Expression="1"/>
    <Text Label="Options:" Type="select"
select="noselection,one,two,three" Selectlabel="Make a selection"/>
    <Text Label="Color:" Type="color" Initial="#E0FFE0" />
    <Initiate Name="Caption.Text" value="Web Page from def" />
</ExtensionObject>
```

Generated QVPP file

```html
<div class="ToolWindow-MainBody" avq="foldOutMenu:." style="overflow:
visible !important; float: left;">
<div class="prop-accordion" avq="accordion:.">

//The title for the first section
    <h3 class="prop-h3 accordion-shadow">
        <a href="#">My website</a>
    </h3>
<div class="prop-grid_container accordion-shadow-enabler"
style="overflow:auto;">
<div class="prop-grid_clear prop-grid_top-vertical-spacer-12px prop-
grid_last"></div>

//Label for Dimension 1
    <div class='prop-grid_clear prop-grid_prepend-1 prop-grid_span-5'
avq='prop_label'>My Dimension 1</div>

//Definition of Dimension 1 field
```

```
<div class='prop-grid_span-10 prop-grid_last'>
    <div class='prop-grid_span-7'
avq='prop_dynamicDropdown:.Chart.Dimension.0.Field'></div>
    <div class='prop-width-28px' propicontype='tool'
avq='prop_dlgbuttonjqui:.Chart.Dimension.0:ExtensionDimDialog.qvpp'></di
v>
</div>

<br />
    <div class='prop-grid_clear prop-grid_prepend-1 prop-grid_span-5'
avq='prop_label'>Measure</div>
    <div class='prop-grid_span-10 prop-grid_last'>

//This is the definition for the measure
    <div class='prop-grid_span-7 prop-grid_last' style='width:94%;'
avq='prop_editexpression:.Chart.Expression.0.0.Definition'></div>
    </div><br />

//Label for URL field
    <div class='prop-grid_clear prop-grid_prepend-1 prop-grid_span-5'
avq='prop_label'>Url</div>

//Definition of URL field
    <div class='prop-grid_span-10 prop-grid_last'>
    <div class='popup-grid_span-7 popup-grid_last' style='width:94%;'
avq='prop_editexpression:.Chart.Text.0.Content'></div>
    </div>
<br />

//Checkbox label
<div class='prop-grid_clear prop-grid_prepend-1 prop-grid_span-5'
avq='prop_label'>Checkbox example</div>

//Definiton of Checkbox
    <div class='prop-grid_span-10 prop-grid_last'>
    <div class='prop-grid_clear prop-grid_span-1'
avq='prop_checkbox:.Chart.Text.1.Content'></div>
    </div><br />

//Dropdownlist label
    <div class='prop-grid_clear prop-grid_prepend-1 prop-grid_span-5'
avq='prop_label'>Options:</div>

//Defintion of Dropdownlist
    <div class='prop-grid_span-10 prop-grid_last'>
        <select style='width:94%;' avq='mySelect:.Chart.Text.2.Content'>
            <option value='noselection'>Make a selection</option>
            <option value='one'>one</option>
            <option value='two'>two</option>
            <option value='three'>three</option>
        </select>
    </div><br />
```

```
//Color field label
    <div class='prop-grid_clear prop-grid_prepend-1 prop-grid_span-5'
avq='prop_label'>Color:</div>

//Definiton of Color field
    <div class='prop-grid_span-10 prop-grid_last'>
    <div class='prop-grid_span-1 prop-grid_last'
propicontype='singlecolor'
avq='prop_dlgbutton:.Chart.Text.3.Content:Color.qvpp'></div>
    </div><br />
        </div>

//Standard Properties sections
        <h3 class="prop-h3 accordion-shadow"
avq="activeAccordionHeader:.:GenericPresentationFoldout.qvpp">
            <a href="#">Presentation</a>
        </h3>
        <div class="prop-grid_container accordion-shadow-enabler"
avq="panel::Layout.qvpp"></div>
        <h3 class="prop-h3 accordion-shadow"
avq="activeAccordionHeader::PropertiesCaptionFoldout.qvpp">
            <a href="#">Caption</a>
        </h3>
        <div class="prop-grid_container accordion-shadow-enabler"
avq="panel::Caption.qvpp"></div>
        <h3 class="prop-h3 accordion-shadow"
avq="activeAccordionHeader:.:PropertiesOptionsFoldout.qvpp">
            <a href="#">Options</a>
        </h3>
        <div class="prop-grid_container accordion-shadow-enabler"
avq="panel::Options.qvpp"></div>
    </div>
    <span class="bottom-gap"></span>
</div>
```

Add Javascript to your extension - Script.js

The javascript file (script.js) provides the functionality of your extension.

For example you might want to display a html table or set a variable in your QlikView document, these actions and many more can be achieved within the script.js file.

This is the javascript file for the webpageviewer extension:

```
Qva.AddExtension('QlikView/Examples/WebPageViewer', function() {

    if(!this.framecreated)
    {
        var el = document.createElement("iframe");
        el.setAttribute('id', 'ifrm');
        el.frameBorder = 0; //optional
        el.style.width = this.GetWidth() + "px";
        el.style.height = this.GetHeight() + "px";
        this.Element.appendChild(el);
        el.setAttribute('src', this.Layout.Text0.text);
        this.framecreated = true;
    }
    else
    {
        var ifrm = document.getElementById("ifrm");
        ifrm.style.width = this.GetWidth();
        ifrm.style.height = this.GetHeight();
        ifrm.setAttribute('src', this.Layout.Text0.text);
    }
});
```

This javascript calls the AddExtension method to register the javascript function for the extension called 'QlikView/Examples/WebPageViewer'. Note that the name of the extension in the AddExtension method is relative to the Object folder:

%UserProfile%\AppData\Local\QlikTech\QlikView\Extensions\Objects

This function checks to see if an iframe html object has been created (if not it creates an iframe object) and then sets the 'src' attribute using the first text element in the properties (this.Layout.Text0.text) which contains the URL.

Path to extension directory

Qva.Remote is the path to the webpage:
http://your_qlikview_server/QvAjaxZfc/QvsViewClient.aspx

This can be used to create a path to the extension folder, for example:

`var` extension_path = Qva.Remote + "?public=only&name=Extensions/myextension/";

This is useful when you need to reference files such as images and css files in the extension folder, for example:

this.Element.innerHTML =

 "<div onclick=alert(\'onclick\'); style='width=149px; height:31px;background-repeat: no-repeat; background-image:url(" + extension_path+ "button_image.jpg)'></div>";

In this example the variable extension_path is used to reference an image called button_image.jpg which is in the extension folder. This image displays an alert message when clicked using a html div element.

Register your extension

To register an extension we can use the addextension method.

Remembering to set the path relative to the Object folder for Object extensions. The format is:

Qva.AddExtension('my_new_extension_name', **function()**{...extension javascript..});

The example used in the webpageview example is:

Qva.AddExtension('QlikView/Examples/WebPageViewer', **function()**{...});

Add css stylesheets

Add a style sheet to your extension using the LoadCSS method, for example:

Qva.LoadCSS(extension_path + "style.css");

For example:

1. Backup the script.js of your current custom extension or create a new extension by copying the webpageviewer extension to another folder for this example.   If you create a new extension remember to update the AddExtension method in the script.js to have the correct extension name.

2. Create the following style.css in the extension directory:

```css
body
{
    font-family: "Segoe UI", Tahoma, Geneva, Verdana, sans-serif;
}


h1
{
    font-size: 21pt;
    background-color: gray;
    font-weight: normal;
}

h2
{
    font-size: 12pt;
    font-weight: normal;
}
```

3. Alter the script.js file in the extension folder to reference the stylesheet file:

```javascript
Qva.AddExtension('testext', function() {
var path = Qva.Remote + "?public=only&name=Extensions/testext/";
Qva.LoadCSS(path+"style.css");

this.Element.innerHTML =
 "<div><H1>This is the main title</H1></br><h2>This is some other
text</h2></div>";
});
```

4. This should create an extension object which looks like the following screenshot:

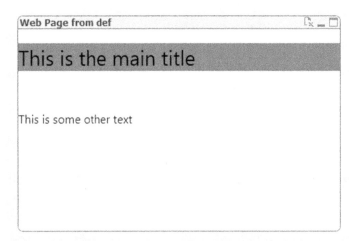

5. Now you can alter the css file and press F5 to refresh extension to see your changes.

Add script files - JQUERY

Jquery is a javascript library designed to make doing things like animation and ajax much easier. In a similar way to adding css files to your extension you can add scripts such as jquery as shown:

```
function onDoneLoadingScripts()
{
        alert("DONE");
}
Qva.LoadScript(extension_path + 'jquery.js', onDoneLoadingScripts );
```

In this example the function onDoneLoadingScripts() is called once the jquery file has been loaded.

Full jquery example script.js file:

```
var doc;
function onDoneLoadingScripts()
{
//      alert("DONE");
}

function init() {
 doc = Qv.GetCurrentDocument();

Qva.LoadScript("/QvAjaxZfc/QvsViewClient.aspx?public=only&name=Extension
s/Examples/WebPageViewer/jquery.js", onDoneLoadingScripts);
if(!jQuery)
        alert("Essential plugin (jquery) not loaded");
}

Qva.AddExtension('QlikView/Examples/WebPageViewer',function() {

this.Element.innerHTML = "<H1>TEST JQUERY</H1>"+
                "<h2>This is a heading</h2>"+
                "<p>This is a paragraph.</p>"+
                "<p>This is another paragraph.</p>"+
                "<button>Click me</button>";

$(document).ready(function(){
        $("button").click(function(){
                $("p").hide();
                        });
                        });
}, false);
init();
```

1. Add the jquery.js file to the extension folder.

2. In this example you can see from the name in the AddExtension method that we have alerted the webpageviewer example extension.

3. The extension will look like the following screenshot:

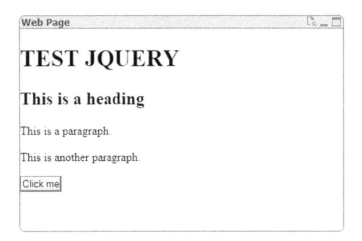

4. When you click on the 'Click Me' button the jquery in the script.js will have the effect of hiding the <p> elements as shown:

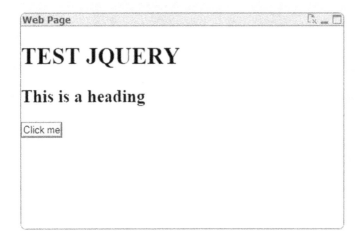

How to Reference fields

Next we will look at how to reference fields defined in the extension properties or the data associated with the extension.

Text\checkbox fields

To get the value of the first text\checkbox field:

this.Layout.Text0.text.toString();

The second text field would use Text1 instead of Text0 and so on.To access the data for a particular object we use the following statement:

var table_data = this.Data;

In the next example we will show how to read and display the data from a qlikview chart object using the javascript of an extension.

Values in a table

1. To retrieve the data that is used in the extension object we will load customer data used in previous examples, setup the extension object with a dimension and expression and read the data from the table in the script.js file.

2. You may remember earlier in the chapter we mention that the object extensions are based on chart objects.

3. Add the following script to the loadscript:

    ```
    customer_data:
    LOAD Product,
        Customer,
        [Qtr 1],
        [Qtr 2],
        [Qtr 3],
        [Qtr 4]
    FROM
    [SampleCustomerReports.xls]
    (biff, embedded labels, table is [Source Data$]);
    ```

4. Make sure that the SampleCustomerReports.xls file is in the same folder as the new QlikView document.

5. Reload the document.

6. Create a copy of the webpageviewer extension or backup and alter the current extension you are customizing.

7. Turn on the webview, right click on the sheet, select New sheet object' and add your extension to the sheet.

8. Select the Settings->Sheet Properties->Objects tab.

9. Select the Object that represents the extension. If there is only 1 object on the sheet this will be ObjectID CH01 and if it is the web page viewer it will also have a caption of 'Web Page'. Then click the Properties button.

10. The Chart properties dialog box should appear. Add a dimension of customer and an expression of =sum([Qtr 1])

11. Edit the script.js file of the extension you are customizing to use the following code: Remember: To change the path to the extension in the AddExtension method.

```
Qva.AddExtension('QlikView/Examples/WebPageViewer',
     function() {

//Get the data from the chart in the qlikview document
 var table_data = this.Data;
 html_string = "<H1>HTML TABLE TEST</H1>";

for(var x = 0; x < 5; x++) {
                   var current_row = table_data.Rows[x];
//Get the value of the first dimension
                   var dim1 = current_row[0].text;
//Get the value of the expression:
                   var expr = current_row[1].text;
//Add the values to the html string
                   html_string += "dim1: " + dim1 + " expression: " +
expr + "<br />";
}

//Add the full html string to the extension in the qlikview document
 this.Element.innerHTML = html_string;
           }, false);
```

When you refresh the extension it should look like the following screenshot:

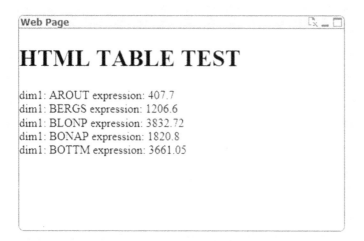

We have limited this example to 5 rows, to get the full number for rows in a table use the following variable:

table_data.Rows.length

```
so the for loop in the script would start:

for(var x = 0; x < table_data.Rows.length; x++)
{
<commands in the loop>
}
```

Create your own functions

Next we will cover 2 ways you can create your own javascript functions

To create a function with a single parameter :

```
function myfunction(myvar)
{
      alert("parameter 1 is "+myvar);
}
```

This function simply displays an alert message using the parameter passed to the function as part of the message to be displayed.

The statement below calls the function 'myfunction' passing the parameter of ' customer1' :

myfunction('customer1');

Callback functions

If you need to create a function to be used as a callback function. For example a function that is called after a jquery script library has been called or to call a function when an object is updated .

For example, create the simple callback function using the function below:

```
var callbackfunction = function () {
    alert("callback - done");
};
```

You can then assign the fuction called callbackfunction to the object CH01 (the first chart object) using the GetObject method:

```
var doc = Qv.GetCurrentDocument();
doc.GetObject('CH01', callbackfunction);
```

This callback function will be called anytime the object CH01 is updated.

Add an image button

In this example we will add an image button using css to the extension and assign a alert message.

NOTE: The differences between the paths to the extension folder between the AddExtension method

QlikView/Examples/WebPageViewer and the name parameter of the path variable which is:

name=Extensions/QlikView/Examples/WebPageViewer/

The full script.js is next:

```
Init = function() {
    doc = Qv.GetCurrentDocument();
}
//Register the extension
Qva.AddExtension('QlikView/Examples/WebPageViewer', function() {
 var doc;
```

//Get the pathof the extension folder. This is the location of where the image used for the button should be stored.

```
var path = Qva.Remote +
"?public=only&name=Extensions/QlikView/Examples/WebPageViewer/";

//This function creates an html div object and uses css to set the
background image using the
//clickme.png file and assigns and alert message to the onclick event.

var path = Qva.Remote +
"?public=only&name=Extensions/QlikView/Examples/WebPageViewer/";
        this.Element.innerHTML = "<div onclick=alert(\'onclick\');
style='width=149px; height:60px;background-repeat: no-repeat;
background-image:url("+path+
"clickme.png)'></div>";
Init();
});
```

If you are using the image file downloaded in the source code this extension should look like the following screenshot :

If you click on the image the alert message defined in the script.js file will be displayed.

QlikView variables

We have already shown how to get data from the qlikview document and display it in the extension.

1. Next we will show how you can easily set the values of variables in the QlikView document using javascript code in the extension.

2. In this example you need to update the defintion.xml to the following code:

```
<?xml version="1.0" encoding="utf-8"?>
<ExtensionObject Label="PostData" Description="">
 <Text Label="show_website_status" Initial=""
Expression="=show_website_status"/>
</ExtensionObject>
```

3. This will create a textbox called show_website_status that can be referenced in the script.js file as this.Layout.Text0.text because it is the first textbox (Text0).

4. The Script.js is updated to the following code.

```
var doc;
var done_once;
function init() {
  doc = Qv.GetCurrentDocument();
}
Qva.AddExtension('QlikView/Examples/WebPageViewer',
      function() {
                  var state = this.Layout.Text0.text;
                  if(state == "False" && done_once!="true")
                  {
                          alert('set show_website_status to TRUE');

        doc.SetVariable("show_website_status","TRUE");
                          done_once = "true";
                  }
            }, false);
init();
```

5. This script file gets the current value of the show_website_status textbox and sets it to the variable state. This the state variable has the value 'False' then and alert message is displayed and the qlikview variable show_website_status is set to TRUE using the SetVariable method.

6. The SetVariable method takes 2 parameters. This first one is the name of the qlikview variable in double quotes and the second is the string you wish to set the variable to.

7. The SetVariable method is part of the Qv.Document class, because of this we need to created an object of the Qv.Document class using the following code :

```
doc = Qv.GetCurrentDocument();
```

8. Then we can call the SetVariable method using the doc variable:

```
doc.SetVariable("show_website_status","TRUE");
```

9. Next, add the QlikView variable show_website_status to your QlikView document by selecting Settings->Variable Overview, click the add button and enter the variable name show_website_status.

10. When you add or refresh the extension you are working on the alert message will be displayed and the variable show_website_status will be set to TRUE.

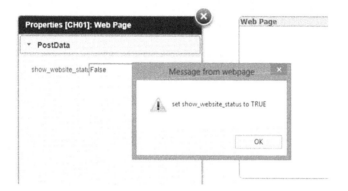

11. We added the done_once variable to prevent the javascript from trying to set the variable multiple times. The SetVariable method is very useful for providing some interaction between the qlikview document and extension.

The Extensions on the server

Windows 2008

To use your QlikView Extension on a QlikView Server you will need to copy your Extension from:

%UserProfile%\AppData\Local\QlikTech\QlikView\Extensions\

 folder to the following folder:

%ProgramData%\QlikTech\QlikViewServer\Extensions

Within the extensions folder if the objects or the documents folder does not already exist. They will need to be created so that you have the same structure under the extensions folder as on your development machine.

Summary

Creating extensions can open your qlikview document to using standard web development languages such as jquery or integrating your qlikview document data with google maps.

This completes section 1 in which we focused on the User Interface aspects of QlikView development.

In the next section will cover how to manage your qlikview data for effectively and cover advanced topics such as how to access data from your own custom data sources.

Section 2: QlikView Data

Managing the QlikView Data Model

Only use the data you need.

In QlikView the schema is critical – a selection in QlikView affects the whole schema. Therefore you need to develop the load script with the end in mind.

Try to keep the complexity in the load scripts and away for the GUI this will improve the performance of your document especially in a working environment.

If the data model is correct it should make the development of the GUI easier.

This is even more important if you have separate design teams that will be using your data.

Also it is more time consuming to copy complex expressions into several sheet objects and the maintenance of changes to those expressions.

If there are some tables\fields that you only require while creating the QVD you can drop these after they have been used using the drop command to reduce any data that is not required, for example:

DROP TABLE tablename
DROP FIELD fieldname

Fact and Dimension tables

Fact tables contain the values that the expressions will be based on. For example a fact table for a dimensional model based on product orders might contain fields such as the amount the order costs and any discounts\taxes.

Whereas the dimension tables would contain values used to select records in the fact table. For example common dimension tables are a calendar dimension table which would allow the selection of months\years, a country dimension table and a sales person dimension table.

Dimension tables connect to the fact table using key fields.

One method is to manage and create reusable dimension tables is to create a QVD for each Dimension table. This will be covered later in this section.

Star schema

Star schema arranges the dimension tables around a central fact table that contains the measures.

The dimension tables arranged around a central fact table that contains the measures.

Each dimension is only one table.

The dimension tables are used to selections for example a list of customer names.

Whereas the fact table contains the details that will be used in calculations for example order amount details.

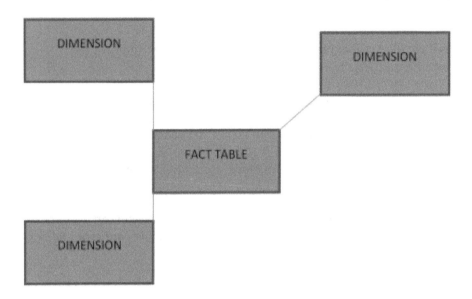

Snowflake schema

Like Star schema but the dimensions are normalized into several tables. When tables are normalized this means that they have been organized using rules called normal forms in such a way to reduce duplication of data and try to organized the data in a logical fashion.

Link Tables

1. Sometimes called dimensional link tables.

2. Link tables are commonly used to solve problems such as:

    a. To remove Circular references \ synthetic keys and tidy your data model.

    b. Multiple fact tables – the usual example is when comparing budget and actual data which you wish to keep the fact tables seperate.

    c. To create links between tables where links do not already exist. For example by combining 2 fields and using the autonumber function to create a key. Using autonumber to create keys has the added benefit of using less memory, for example:

        Load Autonumber(ProductID&'-'&OrderID) as %ProdOrderKey
        ProductID,
        OrderID
        From sometable;

Using linked tables are an alternative to concatenating two tables one and having a field to indicate which table the record originally belonged to.

To create a Link Table to 2 fact tables you need to:

1. Concatenate keys used to link to the fact and dimension tables into 1 table.

2. All tables should have a unique key.

3. Use Autonumber to save space on long keys.

4. Break any existing links between tables so that you don't get synthetic keys or circular references.

Link Table Example

For this example we will alter a qlikview document that is being used to track the users spending in various categories such as Food and Coffee to add budgets for each Category\Month.

1. Download the sample data 'Track Your Spending Sample Data' from the practical-qlikview.com download page and add budget data to spreadsheet in a sheet called budget, for example:

Month	Food	Petrol	Coffee	Clothes
Jan	100	50	20	30
Feb	100	50	20	30
Mar	100	50	20	30

2. Add the following loadscript:

```
For Each Sheetname in 'Jan$','Feb$','Mar$'

    track_spending:
    CrossTable(Category, Amount)
    LOADDate,
    Food,
    Petrol,
    Coffee,
    Clothes
    FROM
    qv_spending_updated.xls
    (biff, embeddedlabels, tableis$(Sheetname));
Next

    budget:
    CrossTable(Category, Amount)
    LOADMonth,
    Food,
    Petrol,
    Coffee,
    Clothes,
    Other
    FROM
    [qv_spending_updated.xls]
    (biff, embeddedlabels, tableis [budget$]);
```

3. The first loop in the script loads all the monthly spending data whereas the second part loads the budget data.

4. This gives a synthetic key - multiple keys between the 2 tables.

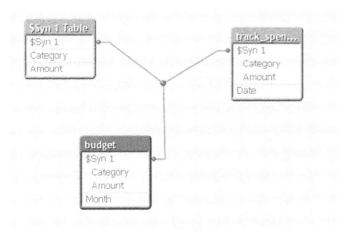

5. Alter the loadscript to create a link table to match the script below.

   By creating the dimension tables which are used for selections , the link table and the fact tables you will remove the synthetic keys from the data model.

//Load the data for the worksheets called Jan, Feb and Mar
for Each *Sheetname* in 'Jan$','Feb$','Mar$'

track_spending:
CrossTable(Category, Amount)
LOAD Date,
Food,
Petrol,
Coffee,
Clothes
FROM
qv_spending_updated.xls
(biff, embedded labels, table is *$(Sheetname)*);
Next

//Load the budget worksheet
budget:
CrossTable(Category, Amount)
LOAD Month,
Food,

```
Petrol,
Coffee,
Clothes,
Other
FROM
[qv_spending_updated.xls]
(biff, embedded labels, table is [budget$]);

// This mapping table is used to convert the numeric value of the month into the short string
// for the month
MonthMap:
MAPPING
LOAD * INLINE [
  Num, Name
  1, Jan
  2, Feb
  3, Mar
  4, Apr
  5, May
  6, Jun
  7, Jul
  8, Aug
  9, Sep
  10, Oct
  11, Nov
  12, Dec
];

//Create the Dimension Tables
dim_category:
LOAD distinct Category
Resident track_spending;
LOAD Category
Resident budget
WHERE NOT Exists(Category);

//Month Dimension - in this example we are loading the months from the track_spending
table and the budget table
dim_month:
NoConcatenate LOAD distinct
ApplyMap('MonthMap', month(Date)) as Month
Resident track_spending;

LOAD Month
```

Resident **budget**;

```
//KEY: Budget\Actual - Month - Date - Category
link_table:
LOAD distinct
Category
,Month
,'Budget' & '-' &Month& '-' &  '$(ANY)' & '-' &Category as %link_key
Resident budget;

LOAD distinct
Category
,ApplyMap('MonthMap', month(Date)) as Month
,'Actual' & '-' &  '$(ANY)' & '-' &month(Date)& '-' &Category as %link_key
Resident track_spending;

//Fact tables
fact_budget:
LOAD
Amount
,'Budget' & '-' &Month& '-' &  '$(ANY)' & '-' &Category as %link_key
,'Budget' as Type
Resident budget;

LOAD
Amount
,'Actual' & '-' &  '$(ANY)' & '-' &month(Date)& '-' &Category as %link_key
,'Actual' as Type
Resident track_spending;

//Remove the original tables
DROP TABLE track_spending;
DROP TABLE budget;
```

6. If you are using this script downloaded from the practical-qlikview.com download page or copying from the book remember to change the name of the excel spreadsheet and the sheet names if your sample data is different.

7. Now you can create a simple table to display the data in the dimension and fact tables and add the category and month fields as listboxes for selection as shown in the screenshot.

Category		Month	
Clothes		Apr	
Coffee		Aug	
Food		Dec	
Other		Feb	
Petrol		Jan	

529.99   🖳 XL ▬ ▢

Category	Month	Type	Actual	Budget
	Jan		100	30
	Feb		50	30
	Mar		19.99	30
	Apr		-	30
	May		-	30
	Jun		-	30
Clothes	Jul		-	30
	Aug		-	30
	Sep		-	30
	Oct		-	30
	Nov		-	30
	Dec		-	30

Joining tables

What are table joins?

Table joins allow you to combine **columns** of data from different tables.

Table joins check if there are rows that match between 2 tables based on matching field names.

As normal in QlikView you have to make sure you only have 1 field in common in both tables otherwise you will get synthetic tables.

If you have written sql statements before you will have almost certain come across table joins and will have no problem in understanding joins in QlikView.

Remember:

Joins add columns whereas concatenation adds Rows

Why use joins?

The most common reason to use sql joins is to reduce the number of tables in your data model.

Alternatives to using joins in qlikview are:

1. ApplyMap and Mapping tables to add a field to the table.

2. Joining the tables in the SQL SELECT statement or a sql stored procedure.

Join types

Default is a full outer join.

To demonstrate how the different join options work we will used the following inline tables:

```
//2 tables
Users:
LOAD * INLINE [
       Name, Department
       User1,Dept1
       User2,Dept2
       User3,Dept3
       ];
```

Managers:
LOAD * INLINE [
        Department, Manager
        Dept1, Manager1
        Dept2, Manager2
        Dept4, Manager4
        ];

The key that links the two tables is 'Department' and there are departments that are in both tables as well as a department that is only in the Users\Managers table.

Inner Join

INNER JOIN will only display records where there is a matching record in each table.

In this example we will join the Users table with the Managers table, the finished table called 'inner_join_table' will contain all the fields in the Users table and the Department field from the Managers table where the Department field matches.

Add the following code to your loadscript:

inner_join_table:

//The Noconcatenate option is to prevent the table being concatenated with the inline table.
NoConcatenate
LOAD
        Name
        ,Department
Resident **Users;**

// Inner join - If no tablename is specified then the previously created table is used for the join.
// In this case the join statement: inner join (inner_join_table)
// would have given the same result.
inner join
LOAD
        Manager
        ,Department
Resident Managers;

//We drop the orginal inline tables so that we don't create synthetic keys.
drop tables Users,Managers;

When you reload the loadscript , check the table viewer (CTRL+T) you can preview the data which should be the same as the screenshots below:

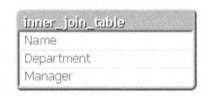

Department	Name	Manager
Dept1	User1	Manager1
Dept2	User2	Manager2

Outer Join

An outer join allows rows that do not match to still be included in the final table.

The 'outer join' will combine all rows from both tables whether they are matching or not.

Comment out the previous join example and add the following code:

```
outer_join_table:
NoConcatenate
LOAD
        Name
        ,Department
Resident Users;

outer join (outer_join_table)
LOAD
        Manager
        ,Department
Resident Managers;

drop tables Users,Managers;
```

When you reload the document and look at the table viewer you should see the following single table:

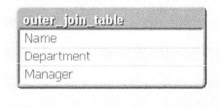

If you preview right click on the table and select preview you will see the following data that shows the combination of all rows from both User and Manager tables as shown:

Department	Name	Manager
Dept1	User1	Manager1
Dept2	User2	Manager2
Dept3	User3	-
Dept4	-	Manager4

Left Outer Join

When joining tables together the first table that is part of the join is also known as the left table, whereas the second table used is known as the right table. In this example:

LEFT TABLE = Users table

RIGHT TABLE = Managers table

If you change the following line in the previous example:

outer join (outer_join_table)

to

left join (outer_join_table)

Then reload the document the data will have changed to:

In this example all the rows in the first table which is the Users table have been included and only matching rows in the second (Managers) table.

Department	Name	Manager
Dept1	User1	Manager1
Dept2	User2	Manager2
Dept3	User3	-

RIGHT OUTER JOIN

A right outer join is simply the opposite of a left outer join, where all the rows of the right table are listed.

Change the left outer join to a right outer join by making the following change:

> left join (outer_join_table)
> to
> right join (outer_join_table)

Reload the document and you will see that the Managers table which is the right table in this example is the one has all the rows listed.

Department	Name	Manager
Dept1	User1	Manager1
Dept2	User2	Manager2
Dept4	-	Manager4

Keep

The Keep option is similar to JOIN but does not merge the tables.

The rows are removed in the same way as a join but the tables remain seperate.

This is a useful option when you just want to reduce the data in the tables but not actually change the structure of your data model.

Inner Keep Example

Users_table:
NoConcatenate
LOAD   Name,Department Resident Users;

Managers_table:
inner keep LOAD Manager,Department Resident Managers;

drop tables Users,Managers;

When you reload the document and view the tables if will appear as if nothing has changed.

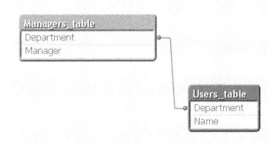

If you preview the data in the tables you will see that only matching rows remain in the tables as shown in the screenshots of each table below:

Managers_table:

Department	Manager
Dept1	Manager1
Dept2	Manager2

Users_table:

Department	Name
Dept1	User1
Dept2	User2

Summary

Using joins you can create a cleaner data model which in turn will make the creation of your user interface easier to develop and maintain.

Next we will cover qvds and various techniques for improving the performance when creating qvds.

2. QVD - QlikView Data

Why use QVDs?

There are several reasons for using QVDs the main ones being:

1. You will read the data into your document faster (**FASTER**).

2. You can create incremental loads of data where you only read the records from the data sources that have changed (**LESS DATA READ**).

3. You can reuse the QVDs in multiple documents (**REUSE MEANS EASIER AND FASTER DEVELOPMENT**).

Next we will cover several different ways in which you can use QVDs.

Using the STORE command

The STORE command can save a full table into a qvd:

Using the format:

STORE <table> INTO <qvd filename including path>.qvd (qvd);

For example:

STORE backup_info INTO C:\backup_info.qvd (qvd);

This command will store the table called backup_info into the c:\backup_info.qvd file.

QVD Incremental Loading

In this example we will cover an example of how to using incremental loading with QVDs.

Using the incremental loading technique when creating QVD files means that you will have to read only the data that has changed.

If you only need to add\delete rows to the QVD file a Unique field such as an ID field which is

an integer is all that is required.

If you need to update rows from the QVD you will require a modification datetime field.

Initial QVD Load

1. Create the initial qvd file using the following loadscript:

```
SET vCreateInitialQVD=1;

// Create the inital QVD
IF vCreateInitialQVD=1 THEN

users:
LOAD id,
    username,
    [license type],
    created,
    modified
FROM
C:\inc_qvd.xls
(biff, embedded labels, table is [Sheet1$]);

IF ScriptErrorCount=0 then

        //Save the table into a qvd file
        STORE users into c:\users.qvd(qvd);
END IF
END IF
```

As an alternative to using a variable set to 0\1 to determine whether or not to create the qvd with an inital load or incremental load you could use a function such as QvdCreateTime to check if the qvd file exists and only perform the inital load if the qvd does not exist.

The inital qvd load should contain the following data which you can create in a spreadsheet yourself or download from the practical-qlikview.com download page.

id	username	license type	created	modified
1	UserA	Named	01/04/2012	
2	UserB	Document	01/01/2013	
3	UserC	Document	05/06/2013	

Incremental Load Example

1. Now that we have created the base qvd file with the inital load we will add the code to perform the incremental load.

2. In this example we will explain how we add just the new records added to the excel spreadsheet.

NOTE: incremental load is covered in an IF statement so only either the incremental load or base load is run when the document is reloaded.

3. The processes to perform an incremental load just for appended records is simply:

    a. Load the current QVD file.

    b. Find out the created date of the last record in the excel spreadsheet.

    c. Only read the records from the spreadsheet that have a date greater than the last created date in the QVD.

    d. Concatenate the rows read from the current qvd and the new records read from the spreadsheet.

    e. Save the concatenated table into the qvd.

In this example we have added the extra row to the spreadsheet (username 'Mark'), as shown below:

Id	Username	license type	created	modified
1	UserA	Named	01/04/2012	
2	UserB	Document	01/01/2013	
3	UserC	Document	05/04/2013	
4	Mark	Named	06/05/2013	

```
//Do the incremental load
IF vCreateInitialQVD=0 THEN

//Load the current qvd file
users:
LOAD * FROM c:\users.qvd(qvd);

//Get the date of the last record created - assuming they are in date order
LET user_created_maxdate = timestamp(Peek('created',-1),'DD/MM/YYYY');
DROP TABLE users;

//Load the records that have been added
noconcatenate users:
 LOAD id,
    username,
    [license type],
    created,
    modified
FROM C:\inc_qvd.xls
(biff, embedded labels, table is [Sheet1$])
where created > '$(user_created_maxdate)';

// Load records that have not been updated from the qvd
UNQUALIFY *;
users:
Concatenate LOAD *
 FROM c:\users.qvd(qvd);
IF ScriptErrorCount=0 then
        STORE users into c:\users.qvd(qvd);
END IF
END IF
```

4. In the Settings - User Preferences - General tab , check the option:Keep Progress Open after Reload so that you can see that only the appended row is read from the spreadsheet.

5. When you reload the document the following output in the 'Script Execution Progress' screen:

users << users (qvd optimized) 3 lines fetched
users << Sheet1$ 1 lines fetched
users << users (qvd optimized) 4 lines fetched

6. From this you can see that:

3 lines where read from the current qvd,

1 line was read from the spreadsheet - this is the line that was added to the spreadsheet.

4 lines fetched - this is the result of concatenating the qvd and new records read from the spreadsheet.

Updated Rows

To change the incremental load script to read rows that have been updated you need to have a modified date\time field in your spreadsheet.

There are 2 changes required:

1. Start using the modified date\time field instead of the created date\time field to read new records from the spreadsheet.

2. Add the following command to the final qvd load so that only records not changed are read from the qvd:

WHERE NOT Exists(id name);

So that the final concatenation of the qvd and updated records from the spreadsheet will now be:

users:
Concatenate **LOAD** *
 FROM c:\users.qvd(qvd)

WHERE NOT Exists(id);

The full example is:

```
//Do the incremental load
IF vCreateInitialQVD=0 THEN

//Load the current  qvd file
users:
LOAD * FROM c:\users.qvd(qvd);

//Get the date of the last record created - assuming they are in date order
LET user_modified_maxdate = timestamp(Peek('modified',-1),'DD/MM/YYYY');
DROP TABLE users;

//Load the records that have been added
noconcatenate users:
 LOAD id,
    username,
    [license type],
    created,
    modified
FROM
C:\inc_qvd.xls
(biff, embedded labels, table is [Sheet1$])
where created > '$(user_modified_maxdate)';

////Load records that have not been updated from the qvd
////This can be taken from the QVD or Resident table
UNQUALIFY *;
users:
Concatenate LOAD *
 FROM c:\users.qvd(qvd)

  WHERE NOT Exists(id);

IF ScriptErrorCount=0 then
        STORE users into c:\users.qvd(qvd);
END IF
```

Updated Rows Example

1. Add modified dates to the spreadheet so they are the same as the created field as shown:

id	username	license type	created	modified
1	UserA	Named	01/04/2012	01/04/2012
2	UserB	Document	01/01/2013	01/01/2013
3	UserC	Document	05/04/2013	05/04/2013
4	Mark	Named	06/05/2013	06/05/2013

2. Set vCreateInitialQVD=1 and reload the document to refresh the qvd.

3. Modify one of the records and update the modified date field. For example see UserB :

id	username	license type	created	modified
1	UserA	Named	01/04/2012	01/04/2012
2	UserB	Named	01/01/2013	07/05/2013
3	UserC	Document	05/04/2013	05/04/2013
4	Mark	Named	06/05/2013	06/05/2013

4. Set vCreateInitialQVD=0 and reload the document, you should see the following text in the progress screen if you are using the same data.

   users << users (qvd optimized) 4 lines fetched
   users << Sheet1$ 1 lines fetched
   users << users (qvd optimized) 4 lines fetched

Full loadscript used in this example:

```
//Do the incremental load
IF vCreateInitialQVD=0 THEN

//Load the current
users:
LOAD * FROM c:\users.qvd(qvd);

//Get the date of the last record created - assuming they are in date order
LET user_modified_maxdate = timestamp(Peek('modified',-1),'DD/MM/YYYY');
```

```
DROP TABLE users;

//Load the records that have been added
noconcatenate users:
 LOAD id,
    username,
    [license type],
    created,
    modified
FROM
C:\inc_qvd.xls
(biff, embedded labels, table is [Sheet1$])
where modified > '$(user_modified_maxdate)';

// Load records that have not been updated from the qvd
// This can be taken from the QVD or Resident table
UNQUALIFY *;
users:
Concatenate LOAD *
 FROM c:\users.qvd(qvd)
  WHERE NOT Exists(id);

IF ScriptErrorCount=0 then
        STORE users into c:\users.qvd(qvd);
END IF
END IF
```

Deleted Rows Example

Finally we will alter the loadscript to updated the qvd when rows are deleted from the spreadsheet.

This is simply done by added an inner join command to the spreadsheet so that only rows that match the current spreadsheet are kept in the final table.

```
INNER JOIN
 LOAD id FROM
 C:\inc_qvd.xls
        (biff, embedded labels, table is [Sheet1$]);
```

1. Delete UserA from the spreadsheet

id	username	license type	created	modified
2	UserB	Named	01/01/2013	07/05/2013
3	UserC	Document	05/04/2013	05/04/2013
4	Mark	Named	06/05/2013	06/05/2013

2. Add the inner join statement so your incremental code looks like the code below:

```
//Do the incremental load
IF vCreateInitialQVD=0 THEN

//Load the current
users:
LOAD * FROM c:\users.qvd(qvd);

//Get the date of the last record created - assuming they are in date order
LET user_modified_maxdate = timestamp(Peek('modified',-1),'DD/MM/YYYY');
DROP TABLE users;

//Load the records that have been added
noconcatenate users:
 LOAD id,
    username,
    [license type],
    created,
    modified
FROM
C:\inc_qvd.xls
(biff, embedded labels, table is [Sheet1$])
where modified > '$(user_modified_maxdate)';

// Load records that have not been updated from the qvd
// This can be taken from the QVD or Resident table
UNQUALIFY *;
users:
Concatenate LOAD *
 FROM c:\users.qvd(qvd)
  WHERE NOT Exists(id);

 INNER JOIN
 LOAD id FROM
C:\inc_qvd.xls
```

(biff, embedded labels, table is [Sheet1$]);

IF ScriptErrorCount=0 then
          STORE users into c:\users.qvd(qvd);
END IF
END IF

 Reload the document and check the progress shows same as the text below if you are using the same data. You should note that the last line shows that 1 line less has been read because of the inner join.

users << users (qvd optimized) 4 lines fetched
users << Sheet1$ 1 lines fetched
users << users (qvd optimized) 4 lines fetched
users-1 << Sheet1$ 3 lines fetched

Buffer Statement

This command uses QVDs to buffer the result of the load statement.

This command can be used to improve performance during reloads by reducing the data that needs to be read from the datasource.

For example it can be used with Direct Discovery loadscripts to avoid unnecessary calls back to the database server.

Examples:

Buffer select * from log;

INCREMENTAL - only reads records not read from data sources - updates QVD after.

Buffer (incremental) load * from log;

STALE AFTER - recreates QVD from data source after time limit:

BUFFER (stale after 7 days) load * from log;

In Settings -> User Preferences -> Locations you will see the default location for buffers used by the qlikview desktop application is:

C:\Users\<Your Username>\AppData\Local\QlikTech\QlikView\Buffers

To test this, read in some data from a small text file and add the following buffer command:

NOTE: You will need to use **hours** even for 1 hour or you will get an error message. For example:

buffer (stale after 1 hours)

as shown below:

test_buffer:
buffer (stale after 1 hours)
LOAD @1
FROM
C:\anyoldfile.txt
(txt, codepage is 1252, no labels, delimiter is '\t', msq);

Reload the document and you will see that a qvd file with a long filename such as the one below has been created in the buffer location:

7b68166fa5328b60943bfb382c803e27763bacdd.qvd

QVD optimization

The reason for checking that the qvd load is optimized is that it means you will get a faster load of your data.

You can check if the qvd load is optimized by looking in the script execution progress for the text '(qvd optimized)'. If your table of data is large enough you will probably notice in the time taken to reload the document that optimized.

Your QVD load will not be optimized if there are transformations or filtering except EXISTS in WHERE clause.

Useful QVD functions

QVD and File functions

There are several file functions that can be used to get extra information on files.

We will cover some of the more useful ones next:

The FOR EACH loop can be used in conjunction with the filelist command to loop around a list of files.

filelist(path_to_files)

path_to_files - this is the path to the files to process and can be a string or variable.

This example will process all the qvd files in the folder c:\myfolder

```
FOR EACH vFileName in filelist('c:\myfolder\' & '*.qvd')
....some commands...
NEXT;

LET Last_Updated = today();

FOR EACH FileName in filelist('c:\*.qvd')
                QVDStatus:
                LOAD
                '$(Last_Updated)' as QVD_last_updated,
                Date( QvdCreateTime('$(FileName)') ,'YYYY-MM-DD hh:mm:ss') as
FileTimeStamp,
                QvdNoOfRecords('$(FileName)') as QVD_record_count,
                QvdTableName('$(FileName)') as QVD_table
                AUTOGENERATE 1;
NEXT;
```

CREATE QVDs documents for each table in an existing document

Sometimes you might want to create QVDs for a QlikView document that you have already developed.

Below is a script that uses the BINARY statement to read the data from a QlikView document that you have already created and then create a QVD file for each table in the document:


```
BINARY my_original_dashboard.qvw;

//STORE TABLES AS QVD

SET vDataDir = 'QVD\';

fori=0 to NoOfTables()-1

        LET d= TableName(i);

        STORE $(d) into $(vDataDir)\$(d).QVD;

NEXT

LET j = NoOfTables();

do while j > 0

        let d = TableName(0);

        drop table $(d);

        let j = NoOfTables();

loop
```

Summary

Creating qvds in the most efficient manner possible is an important technique to learn if you intend to develop qlikview documents in a working environment.

Creating QVDs also means that data can easily be shared between qlikview documents if required and only read from the data source the once.

One useful tool for viewing the contents of a qvd quickly is called qviewer the url to try this tool is http://easyqlik.com/.

3. QVX - Custom Data sources

What is QVX?

QVX stand for QlikView Data Exchange and is used for data exchange between a data source and QlikView where you cannot access the data with an OLE DB\ODBC connection..

With QVX you can either:

PERSISTENT FILE - Saved the data to a QVX file which can be read into a qlikview document in a similar way to QVD's.

NAMED PIPE –If you can query the data source from the QVX connector, you can read data into the QlikView document for the connector.

When would you use QVX?

Examples of when you might use QVX are:

1. Reading windows performance counters such as the amount of RAM available on your server.

2. Reading Windows EventLog details.

3. Reading the files in a directory (as we shall see in the example).

If possible using QVD's will still give you better performance over QVX.

We will now cover an example QVX application, although if you do not know c# reading this chapter will not turn you into an expert in c# programming overnight it should show you that creating your own custom data sources need not be a complex task.

QVX Overview

QVX consists of 3 main classes:

Program

This class creates new instance of QvDirectoryListServer which implements QvxServer and passes any arguments that will be used by this class.

QvDirectoryListServer

Returns a class that implements QvxConnection , in this case the class is called QvDirectoryListConnection (CreateConnection method).

CreateConnectionString() - This method returns the text for the connection string used in the loadscript.

QvDirectoryListConnection

Extract the data that will be shown in QlikView - in this example we are getting a directory listing. Then call the MakeEntry method to create a row in the QVX table.

QVX Directory Listing example

QVX requirements

- QlikView version 10 or above

- .NET Framework 4 Client Profile or above

- Microsoft Visual Studio 2010 or above or Visual Studio Express.The examples are developed using Microsoft Visual Studio Express 2012 for Windows Desktop.
  The current url to download this product is below:

  http://www.microsoft.com/visualstudio/eng/products/visual-studio-express-for-windows-desktop

Testing QVX connectors

When testing your QVX connectors in qlikview you will need to copy the connector executable ie: QvDirectoryList.exe and the qvxlibrary.dll into the following folder on your development machine:

C:\Program Files\QlikView

Using QVX on a QlikView server

When installing on server add the files

QvxLibrary.dll and the connector executable such as QvDirectoryList.exe

to:

c:\Program Files (x86)\Common Files\QlikTech\Custom Data\<Connector name>

For example:

c:\Program Files (x86)\Common Files\QlikTech\Custom Data\QvDirectoryList

If it can't be found you will get the following error in the log file :

 CUSTOM CONNECT*Provider*QvEventLogConnectorSimple.exe*XUserId*XPassword*

21/09/2012 13:10:33:   Error: Invalid custom connector QvEventLogConnectorSimple.exe.dll

21/09/2012 13:10:33:   Used QVConnect: C:\Program Files\QlikView\Distribution Service\QvConnect64.EXE

21/09/2012 13:10:33:   General Script Error

21/09/2012 13:10:33:   Execution Failed

21/09/2012 13:10:33:   Execution finished.

Directory Listing Example

The directory listing example will retrieve details of files from a folder parameter past to the connector.

The data for this example could have been retrieved using the FILELIST command in the loadscript. One advantage of using a connector would be if we required to add more complex logic to retrieving the list of files or if the solution was being developed by someone that did not have knowledge of QlikView development.

The full code for this example is available for download from the practical-qlikview.com download page. See comments in the code for more information about the methods.

Program class

```
using System;

using QvDirectoryList;
namespace QvDirectoryConnector
{
    static class Program
    {
        [STAThread]
        static void Main(string[] args)
        {
            if (args != null&&args.Length>= 2)
            {
//Create new instance of QvDirectoryListServer which implements
//QvxServer and pass any arguements

new QvDirectoryListServer().Run(args[0], args[1]);
            }
        }
    }
}
```

The Run() method takes 2 parameters :

Run(string parentString, string pipeName)
parentString – reference to parent window handle
pipeName – Command pipe name.

When no arguments are passed this command is run

new QvDirectoryListServer().RunStandalone("", "StandalonePipe", "", "C:\\test.qvx", "select * from DirectoryFileList");

You can see the RunStandalone() method being called in the context below:

```csharp
using System;
using QvDirectoryList;
namespace QvDirectoryConnector
{
static class Program
{
        [STAThread]
        static void Main(string[] args)
        {
if (args != null&&args.Length>= 2) {

//Create new instance of QvDirectoryListServer which implements
QvxServer and pass any arguements
new QvDirectoryListServer().Run(args[0], args[1]);
}
else
{
    Console.WriteLine("Generate QVX file");
    new QvDirectoryListServer().RunStandalone("", "StandalonePipe", "",
"C:\\test.qvx", "select * from DirectoryFileList");
            }
        }
    }
}
```

QvDirectoryListConnection

The methods covered in the QVDirectoryListConnection are:

1. Init()
    This method defines the structure of the data that will be returned to the qlikview document. For example: the fields are defined using the QvxField class and the table is defined using the QvxTable class.

    The QvxTable class uses the option GetRows to define the method that will be used to return the data to the table, in this example the methods is GetDirectoryFiles().

2. GetDirectoryFiles() The method calls the MakeEntry method once for each file it finds in the c:\ directory.

3. MakeEntry() This method returns a row of data using QvxDataRow() where in this example the first field is set to the filename.

QvDirectoryListConnection

```
using System;
using System.Collections.Generic;
using System.Diagnostics;
using System.Text.RegularExpressions;
using QlikView.Qvx.QvxLibrary;
using System.IO;

namespace QvDirectoryList
{
        internal class QvDirectoryListConnection : QvxConnection
        {

public override void Init()
{
QvxLog.SetLogLevels(true, true);
QvxLog.Log(QvxLogFacility.Application, QvxLogSeverity.Notice, "Init()");

//QVX fields that QlikView can see.
varfileFields = newQvxField[]
  {
        new QvxField("Filename", QvxFieldType.QVX_TEXT,
        QvxNullRepresentation.QVX_NULL_FLAG_SUPPRESS_DATA,
        FieldAttrType.ASCII)
  };

MTables = newList<QvxTable>
{
        new QvxTable
        {
```

```
                //QVX Table name that will appear in QlikView
                TableName = "DirectoryFileList",
                GetRows = GetDirectoryFiles,
                Fields = fileFields
            }
    };
}
```

//Extract the data that will be shown in QlikView - in this example we are getting a directory
listing. Then call the MakeEntry method to create a row in the QVX table

```
private IEnumerable<QvxDataRow>GetDirectoryFiles()
 {

     QvxLog.Log(QvxLogFacility.Application, QvxLogSeverity.Notice,
"GetDirectoryFiles()");


// These are the statements that get the data which will be returned to
// the qlikview document.
// You could start experimenting with your own Qvx application by
// replacing the foreach loop with a single call of the MakeEntry method
// and setting the first parameter to any string you would like.


     string[] dirs = Directory.GetFiles(@"c:\", "*");

     foreach (string dir in dirs)
     {
         yield return MakeEntry(dir as String,
FindTable("DirectoryFileList", MTables));
     }
 }

//Create a new row in the QVX Table
private QvxDataRow MakeEntry(String filename, QvxTable table)
 {
     var row = new QvxDataRow();
     row[table.Fields[0]] = filename;
     return row;
}
}
}
```

QvDirectoryListServer

In the **QVDirectoryListServer** class we override the 2 methods **CreateConnection()** and **CreateConnectionString()**.

```
using QlikView.Qvx.QvxLibrary;
using System.Windows.Forms;

namespace QvDirectoryList
{

internal class QvDirectoryListServer : QvxServer{

//Return class that implements QvxConnection , in this case the class is
called QvDirectoryListConnection.
public override QvxConnection CreateConnection()
{
    return new QvDirectoryListConnection();
}

// This method returns the text for the connection string used in the
// loadscript For example:
// CUSTOM CONNECT TO "Provider=QvDirectoryList.exe;
// myconnectionstring=tester; XUserId=cGKWSXA;XPassword=UPFCMFD;";

public override string CreateConnectionString()
{
QvxLog.Log(QvxLogFacility.Application, QvxLogSeverity.Debug,
"CreateConnectionString()");
return"myconnectionstring=tester";
        }
    }
}
```

QVX logging

Creating logging for your QVX connector is a very useful tool for debugging.

QVXLog.(

        QlikView.Qvx.QvxLibrary.QvxLogFacility **facility**,

        QlikView.Qvx.QvxLibrary.QvxLogSeverity **severity**,

        string **message**

facility = What the post relates it,

There are two different types of logs, or log facilities.

The types are Application and Audit.

severity   = There are four different types of log messages, or log severities.

          The types are Debug, Notice, Warning and Error.

message   = The message that will be logged

The log files will be in the folder:

C:\ProgramData\QlikTech\Custom Data\<Connector Name>\Log

When using the following commands:

QvxLog.SetLogLevels(true, true);

SetLogLevels(<u>bool</u> *logDebug*, **<u>bool</u>** *logWarnings*)

This method sets where the debug and warning log levels are included in the log file or not. Depending on the amount of debug\warning logging you use in your connector you might want to only set both these values to true when required.

The Notice and Error severity levels are always included in the log files.

The following command will set a

QvxLog.Log(QvxLogFacility.Application, QvxLogSeverity.Notice, "Starting Init()");

Summary

If you already know how to program in .net you will not have had much problem with this chapter.

If you are new to visual studio you will probably need to spend time creating basic .net programs before you are totally comfortable creating qvx connectors.

Although it is probably not required for most of your qlikview development tasks with more and more companies using web services to exchange data between systems it is certainly a useful skill to learn.

Next we will look at set analysis in more depth.

4. Set Analysis

In this chapter we are going to cover set analysis in more detail than in the book 'Practical Qlikview'.

To start with we will briefly recap when to use set analysis before continuing to look at some examples in more detail.

Set-analysis is used with aggregation functions ie: functions do something to a set of fields.

For example a function might add up the total of a set of numbers, this would be the sum() function.

Currently QlikView has been using the current selection to decide what is included in this set of numbers when you use the sum() function but you can change the set using set analysis.

We will continue to use the 'tracking your spending' example to demonstrate how you can use set analysis.

A set is defined in curly brackets {}

$ = the current selection in this example this could be one month.

So the sum(Spent) expression = Sum(**{$}** Spent)

Another simple example would be the following expression which will sum the total of the spent field has a category of food:

Sum({ $<Category={Food}> } Spent)

Aggregation functions

When starting to use aggregation functions and set analysis it is useful to create a file with the initial structure of set analysis command. For example:

Sum({ $<Dim1={Value1}> } Field)

You can easily see that using an expression template such as this would save time and reduce mistakes when creating what context expressions, especially those set analysis.

Sample data

Before continuing examples in this chapter you will need to get some sample data that you can use with the following examples of set analysis.

You can download the sample data that will be used in this chapter from the following URL:

http://practical-qlikview.com/Downloads.aspx and select the following link to download the SampleCustomerReports.xls file:

Sample Sales Data - Customer Reports

Wildcards

You can use wildcards such as '*' to replace 1 or more characters.

In this example we will use the following set analysis expression to calculate the sum of Quantity*UnitPrice for all CustomerID's that start with AN.

=sum({1<CustomerID={"AN*"}>}Quantity*UnitPrice)

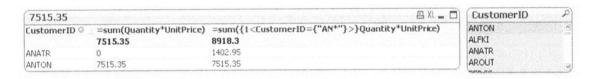

The screenshot above shows a straight table shows 3 columns described below:

Column1 – List of customer ids.

Column 2 – The sum of Quantity * UnitPrice for the current selection.

Column 3 - The sum of Quantity * UnitPrice for the current selection for all records in the document but for only the cutomer ids that are with 'AN'.

You can see that the customerID 'ANTON' has been selected , but because of the set analysis in column 3 the customer starting ANATR and ANTON are also included in the table.

The expression used in column 2 which is =sum(Quantity*UnitPrice) does not include any set analysis and therefore defaults to using the current selection.
Because we are using '1' instead of '$' (the current selection) in our set analysis the expression is not limited to the current selection.

Date Field Example

In this example we will show how you can use date fields with set analysis.

Before the following example change the orders table in your loadscript so that the date fields are converted to dates otherwise the fields will be displayed as numbers.

orders:
LOAD OrderID,
CustomerID,
EmployeeID,
date(OrderDate) asOrderDate,
date(RequiredDate) asRequiredDate,
date(ShippedDate) asShippedDate,
ShipVia,
Freight,
ShipName,
ShipAddress,
ShipCity,
ShipRegion,
ShipPostalCode,
ShipCountry
FROM
[sampledata.xls]
(biff, embeddedlabels, tableis Orders$);

An alternative to making this change in the loadscript would be to set the format of the fields in the Number tab within the document properties.You can also set the formatting for each sheet object but this way will save you some time.

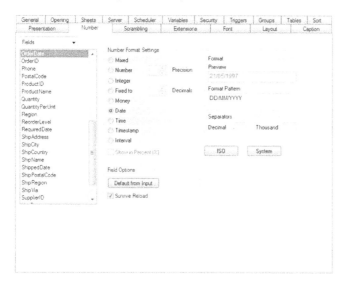

1. In the following example we first create a straight table using the chart sheet object. The dimension will be CustomerID and the expression will be :

   =count(distinct OrderID)

   Your table should look like the following screenshot:

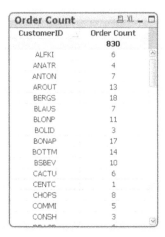

2. Next we will add another column to the table. The new column would calculate the number of orders for each customer after a certain date. The set analysis we will use to make this calculation is displayed below:

   =Count({1 <OrderDate={">=$(=Date('1/1/1998', 'DD/MM/YYYY'))"}>} DISTINCT OrderID)

   This set analysis uses a 1 after the first { to indicate that the current selection will be ignored and counts the distinct OrderID's where the OrderDate is greater that the following expression =$(**=Date('1/1/1998', 'DD/MM/YYYY')**) which is simply the date function surrounded by a dollar expansion $() which simple converts the function into text to use in the set analysis.

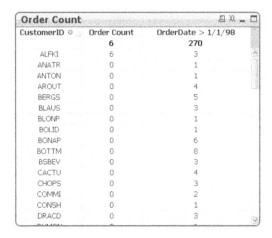

3. If you would like to use set analysis to display a count of orders between two dates you can use the asterix symbol(*) as shown in the next example.

4. In this example we will add an extra column that will display a count of the orders between 1/1/98 and 3/3/98 this:

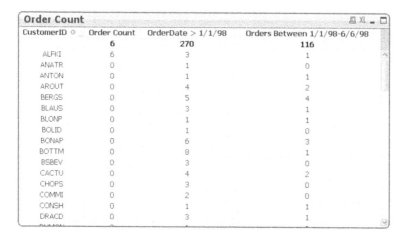

Order Count			
CustomerID	Order Count	OrderDate > 1/1/98	Orders Between 1/1/98-6/6/98
	6	270	116
ALFKI	6	3	1
ANATR	0	1	0
ANTON	0	1	1
AROUT	0	4	2
BERGS	0	5	4
BLAUS	0	3	1
BLONP	0	1	1
BOLID	0	1	0
BONAP	0	6	3
BOTTM	0	8	1
BSBEV	0	3	0
CACTU	0	4	2
CHOPS	0	3	0
COMMI	0	2	0
CONSH	0	1	1
DRACD	0	3	1

=Count({1 <OrderDate= {">=$(=Date('1/1/1998', 'DD/MM/YYYY'))"} *
{"<=$(=Date('3/3/1998', 'DD/MM/YYYY'))"} >} DISTINCT OrderID)

5. The asterix symbol (*) is used to return the records that belong to both sets, in set analysis the asterix symbol is called a set modifier.

Other types of set modifiers are:

+   This will return records that belong to the either set.

-       This will return records that belong to the first set but not the second set.

/   This will return records that only belong to one of the two sets.

6. In this example the two sets are:

Order dates greater than 1/1/1998:

{">=$(=Date('1/1/1998', 'DD/MM/YYYY'))"}

and

Order dates less than 3/3/1998:

{"<=$(=Date('3/3/1998', 'DD/MM/YYYY'))"}

7. If we take one of the sets and look at it in more detail you will see that in mainly consists of the date function:

    =Date('3/3/1998', 'DD/MM/YYYY')

8. Wrapped around the date function is the dollar-sign expansion $().

9. QlikView replaces the function in the dollar sign expansion with the date so the set actually becomes:

    {"<='3/3/1998'"}

10. Using the dollar sign expansion in this way would be more useful if the date 3/3/1998 was replaced with a function such as today() or a variable, for example:

    {"<=$(Today())"}

11. The dollar sign expansion is also useful if you wish to store the function in a variable for example, you could create a variable that contains the following function text:

    =Date('3/3/1998', 'DD/MM/YYYY')

    Then you could replace the function in this set analysis with your variable name.

12. In the example below the variable name that I created was called **vOrderDateLimit**:

    =Count({1 <OrderDate= {">=$(=Date('1/1/1998', 'DD/MM/YYYY'))"} * {"<=$(**vOrderDateLimit**)"} >}   DISTINCTOrderID)

13. It is useful to put set analysis expressions in variables so that if you need to make a change you only need to change the variable rather than every object that uses the expression.

Possible and Excluded values

In this example we will look at using the functions p() and e() in set analysis to return a set of values that are either associated with a particular field or not.

You will see how we can use these functions to build set analysis expressions that will answer more complex queries.

p()

The function p() is used to return the set of possible values associated with another value.

The format of the p() function is: p({set expression} expression)

In the example below this set analysis uses the p() function to count the number of OrderID values for customers that had bought the product 'Chai':

=Count({1<CustomerID=p({1<ProductName={'Chai'}>}CustomerID)>} DISTINCTOrderID)

If we extract the p() function. You will see that the whole expression is basically made up of one set analysis expression within another.

p({1<ProductName={'Chai'}>}CustomerID)

To make the development of such complex expressions easier. It is sometimes useful to test the set expression used in the p() function separately before adding the p() function to a larger set analysis expression.

One simple way to do this is to use the concat function and display the set in a text object as shown below. The seperator of '\n' is used to that each CustomerID is displayed on a new line.

=concat({1<ProductName={'Chai'}>} CustomerID,'\n')

Summary

Set analysis can prove useful to create complex calculations based on various selections in the document. Ideally your documents will contain set analysis only where required especially in charts the performance of your document will be greatly improved if you keep the expressions used as simple as you can and if using charts will large amounts of data force users to make selections first.

Next we will cover various functions and scripting techniques that you can use in your loadscript

5. Scripting - Techniques and Functions

In this chapter we are going to cover various techniques used when scripting in QlikView and also some of the more advanced functions.

Below are listed in the techniques and functions that will be covered in this chapter:

1. Alternate States

2. Preceding Loads

3. File Functions

4. Class

5. Aggr

6. IntervalMatch

7. Date Functions

8. Variables

9. Lookup functions

    a. Lookup

    b. ApplyMap

    c. Exists

    d. Peek

10. Alt

11. RangeSum

Alternate States

Alternate states allow the user to make comparisons between different selections.

For example in the sample data that is being used in this chapter that might be comparing selections between 2 customers.

Using alternate states you can group objects so certain objects only affect objects in the same state.

Alternate State example

1. Download the SampleCustomerReports.xls from the practical-qlikview.com website.

2. Open the SampleCustomerReports.xls spreadsheet , and read the "source data" sheet in using a loadscript such as the one below:

```
customer_data:
  LOAD Product,
     Customer,
     [Qtr 1],
     [Qtr 2],
     [Qtr 3],
     [Qtr 4]
FROM
[SampleCustomerReports.xls]
(biff, embedded labels, table is [Source Data$]);
```

3. Reload your document.

Create the Alternate States

1. Open the Settings->Document properties option. Select the general tab and click on the Alternate States button.

2. Click the Add button and enter a name of 'Customer1', click the add button again and enter a name of 'Customer2'.

3. Click on the OK buttons to close the Alternate states and Document properties screens.

Using the Alternate States

1. By default objects have an 'Alternate State' of <inheritied> , this means that the 'Alternate State' will be the same as the level above.

   For example a sheet object will inherit its alternate state set in the sheet properties.

   You can override the alternate state at the sheet object level if required.

2. Create a new sheet. Then open the Sheet properties, select the general tab, select 'Customer1' from the 'Alternate State' dropdownlist and click the OK button.

3. Create a chart object with a dimension of Customer and expression of =sum([Qtr 1]).

Display the Alternate state used in object title

1. It is useful to identify the state by setting the title to display the state used by the object.

2. Add the following expression to the caption text of your chart.

   =if(StateName()='$', 'Default State', 'State:'&StateName())

3. In the presentation tab of the chart properties check the 'Show partial sums' box and subtotals on top.

Default State	📇 XL _ ☐
Customer	=sum([Qtr 1])
Total	138288.9
AROUT	407.7
BERGS	1206.6
BLONP	3832.72
BONAP	1820.8
BOTTM	3661.05
BSBEV	1714.2
COMMI	216
CONSH	787.6

4. Open the chart properties, general tab and set the Alternate state to Customer1. The title of the chart should change to:

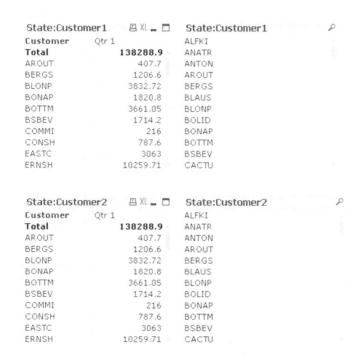

State:Customer1	凰 XL _ ☐
Customer	Qtr 1
Total	**138288.9**
AROUT	407.7
BERGS	1206.6
BLONP	3832.72
BONAP	1820.8
BOTTM	3661.05
BSBEV	1714.2
COMMI	216
CONSH	787.6
EASTC	3063
ERNSH	10259.71

5. Add a listbox using the field of customer and set the alternate state of the list box to be Customer1.

6. Copy both the listbox and chart and in the new copies change the alternate states to Customer2.

7. Add the text =if(StateName()='$', 'Default State', 'State:'&StateName()) to the title of the listboxes so it is easy to identify which alternate state the listboxes are using.

State:Customer1	凰 XL _ ☐		State:Customer1	ₚ
Customer	Qtr 1		ALFKI	
Total	**138288.9**		ANATR	
AROUT	407.7		ANTON	
BERGS	1206.6		AROUT	
BLONP	3832.72		BERGS	
BONAP	1820.8		BLAUS	
BOTTM	3661.05		BLONP	
BSBEV	1714.2		BOLID	
COMMI	216		BONAP	
CONSH	787.6		BOTTM	
EASTC	3063		BSBEV	
ERNSH	10259.71		CACTU	

State:Customer2	凰 XL _ ☐		State:Customer2	ₚ
Customer	Qtr 1		ALFKI	
Total	**138288.9**		ANATR	
AROUT	407.7		ANTON	
BERGS	1206.6		AROUT	
BLONP	3832.72		BERGS	
BONAP	1820.8		BLAUS	
BOTTM	3661.05		BLONP	
BSBEV	1714.2		BOLID	
COMMI	216		BONAP	
CONSH	787.6		BOTTM	
EASTC	3063		BSBEV	
ERNSH	10259.71		CACTU	

8. Now when you select a customer from one of the listboxes it should only affect the chart that has the same alternate state as shown:

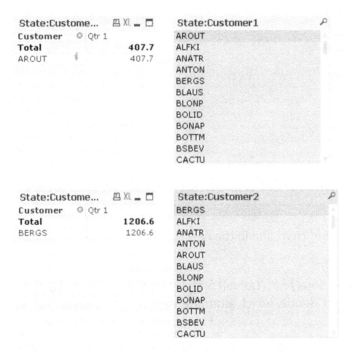

Alternate States and set analysis

1. Using set analyis with alternate states we can create expressions within the same chart that are based on selections from fields that have different alternate states.

   =(SUM({ State1 < [Field1]=[State2]::Field1>} Field_to_sum)

   :: - represent the alternate state in set analysis.

   $:: = default state

2. This examples uses the $:: which is the default state and would therefore display the total of all customers Qtr 1 results.

   =sum({[Customer1]<CustomerID=$::CustomerID>}[Qtr 1])

3. Whereas the this set analysis uses the Customer1 alternate state.

   =sum({[Customer1]<CustomerID=[Customer1]::CustomerID>}[Qtr 1])

   ### Add Set Analysis to the alternate states example

4. In the current example add the following expression to the chart that is using the Alternate state Customer2, with a label of 'Qtr 1 - Customer1 '.

=sum({[Customer1]<CustomerID=[Customer1]::CustomerID>}[Qtr 1])

5. Select 2 different customers for each of the customer listboxes and you will see that the chart that is in alternate state Customer2 now displays totals for the 'Qtr 1' results for the customer selected for the Customer1 and Customer2 alternate states.

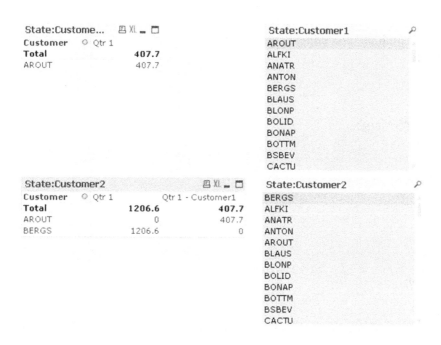

Preceding Loads

Using this technique you can add multiple load statements to perform multiple transformations to the table of data in one go.

In the example below the Margin field is calculated based on the data returned from the load statement below it.

Because you can have multiple preceding loads you can build up quite complex expressions if required.

OrderDetails:

LOAD LineAmt - Cost AS Margin,

*;

LOAD

      LineAmt,

      Margin

SQL SELECT * FROM y;

LEFT JOIN (Orders)

      LOAD OrderID

      SUM(SalesAmt)

RESIDENT OrderDetails

GROUP BY OrderID;

Functions

File Functions

Filelist

Filelist function is used to get a list of files in a directory.

1. In the example below you pass the path to the folder to the filelist directory and use a 'FOR EACH' loop to count the number of files in a folder.

   SET vcount = 0;

   FOR EACH vFileName IN FILELIST ('C:\somefolder*.xls');

   LET vcount = vcount + 1;

   NEXT vFileName;

2. The function dirlist is similar to filelist but instead of files will return the names of folders that exist, for example:

   for each dir in dirlist('C:\filetest*')

   ...Do something

   next dir

Execute

The Execute command can be very useful for executing command line statements during the loadscript. For example creating folders to store qvds, copying files or running other programs.

2 examples below copy a field and create a folder where the name of the folder is in

a variable:

Execute cmd.exe /C copy /Y "..\test_folder\myfile.txt" "..\target_folder \";

Execute cmd.exe /C mkdir "..\somefolder\"$(foldername_variable);

Class

The class function allows you to arrange values into buckets.

1. For example when we add the following inline table to a new qlikview document.

    ```
    values:
    LOAD * INLINE [
      value
      1,
      4,
      7,
      12
    ];
    ```

2. Then add the following table which uses the class function to group by values in the values table into buckets of 5.

    ```
    result:
    LOAD *
    ,class(value,5,'value') as bucket
    Resident  values;
    ```

3. Reload the document and you should see the following result when you preview your data.

4.   You can see from the result table that the class function has identified which range of values (sometimes called a bucket) each value belongs to.

value	bucket
1	0 <= value < 5
4	0 <= value < 5
7	5 <= value < 10
12	10 <= value < 15

    The tableviewer shows the line between the 2 tables:

    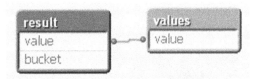

Aggr - Advanced Aggregation

The aggr function allows you to calculate expressions over dimensions.

FORMAT:

aggr([distinct\nodistinct]expression,dimensions)

For example, To sum the total sales amount by country:

aggr(Sum(Sales),Country)

If you add the keyword nodistinct then each combination of dimensions can have 1+ values.

AGGR(nodistinct Sum(Sales),Country)

One problem which the aggr function provides a solution to is the difference between totaling the rows in straight tables compared with pivot tables.

For example:

Total Mode - In pivot tables there is no option to change this in the expression tab.

For straight tables you can change the total mode in the expression tab to be the Sum of the Rows in the table instead of the expression total.

It is important to be aware of this problem with totalling in pivot tables as it may result in a lot of time wasted if it occurs in one of your documents.

The following example will demonstrate the problem and the solution.

1. Create a new qlikview document.

2. Add the following code to your loadscript:

    ```
    aggr_demo:
    LOAD * INLINE [
        User, Amount , Manager
        UserA, 10, Mgr1
        UserB, 20, Mgr2
        UserC, 30, Mgr1
        UserD, 40, Mgr1
    ];
    ```

3. A simple table of data will be created.

4. Create a Straight table using the chart object to display the data.

Manager	User	=sum(Amount)
		100
Mgr1	UserA	10
Mgr2	UserB	20
Mgr1	UserC	30
Mgr1	UserD	40

5. Create a copy of the straight table.

6. Change the chart type to a pivot table, remove the user dimension and change the expression to max(Amount).

Manager	=max(Amount)
Total	40
Mgr1	40
Mgr2	20

7. You can see the total for this pivot table is wrong as it should be 60 instead of 40.

8. Create a copy of this pivot table and change the expression to use the following aggr function:

=sum(aggr(max(Amount),Manager))

9. You will see that the pivot table now displays the correct total as shown:

Manager	=sum(aggr(max(Amount),Manager))
Total	60
Mgr1	40
Mgr2	20

Interval Match

The IntervalMatch function is used to map dates to periods \ slowly changing dimensions.

Interval match has the same functionality as BETWEEN in SQL.

IntervalMatch() creates synthetic tables therefore there is a high RAM\UI performance cost to using this function. One solution to this is to LEFT JOIN the interval match into a parent table to create a cleaner data model.

Next we will demonstrate how to use the interval match function using a simple example.

Interval Match Example

1. Create a new qlikview document and add the following code to the loadscript:

   TabA:

   LOAD * INLINE [

   Time

   1

   2

   3

   4

   5

   6

   7

   8

   9

   10

   ];

TabB:

LOAD * INLINE [

Emp, Start, Stop

1, 2, 6

2, 3, 7

3, 1, 4

4, 2, 10

];

INNER JOIN(TabB)

INTERVALMATCH(Time)

LOAD DISTINCT

      Start,

      Stop

RESIDENT TabB;

2.   The function used is IntervalMatch(Time) where the Time field is used to match between the start and stop interval.

3.   Reload the document and view the tableviewer. You will see that the 2 tables TabA and TabB have been created.

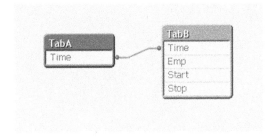

4. The inner join to TabB is required to prevent synthetic tables. If you remove the inner join and reload the document you will get the following table structure:

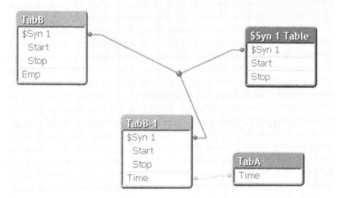

5. Add the inner join back if you removed it and reload the document again.

6. TabA contains the inline table with the time values ranging from 1-10.

7. Preview TabB should display the following data:

Start	Stop	Emp	Time
2	6	1	2
2	6	1	3
2	6	1	4
2	6	1	5
2	6	1	6
2	10	4	2
2	10	4	3
2	10	4	4
2	10	4	5

8. You can see from this data Emp 1,that has a Start value of 2 and Stop value of 6 the Time field goes from 2-6.

Date Functions

There are 2 Date() functions used in qlikview , Date() and Date#():

Date(expression,[format code])

Date() can be used for formatting the date and returning a string.

Date() evaluates the expression as a date string according to the format code if supplied, for example:

=Date(Floor(LocalTime()),'YY-MM-DD')

will return: 13-06-21

Date#(expression,[format code])

Date#() is called an interpretation function and evaluates the expression as a number.

Both these functions return a type of Dual which can means the users can see the date in the correct string format but the numeric version of the date can be used for sorting and comparisions.

NOTE: If there is no format code is uses the operating system date format normally set at the start of the loadscript ie:

```
SET DateFormat='DD/MM/YYYY';
```

DATE and TIME

If the date field includes the time it will not be a whole number

For example:

1. Create a text object and set the text field to:

    =num(today())

2. This will display the current date as a number such as 41431.

    Whereas if you change the formula to use LocalTime() so that the date and time is displayed

=num(LocalTime())

3. You will get a number such as 41431.806331019

4. Remove the num() function to use just LocalTime() and the string will be converted back to the current date\time.

   06/06/2013 19:21:25

5. If you wanted to remove the time from the LocalTime() function you could use the Floor() function which has the effect of rounding down the numeric value of the date\time, then apply the date() function to display the date as a string.

   =Date(Floor(LocalTime()))

6. REMEMBER : Because the date is stored as a string\numeric if you are using timestamp fields you will need to use the formula date(floor(timestampfield)) to remove the time from the field if you need to compare only by dates.

Variables

Most of the time when using variables they will work the way that you expect.

Here will will cover some senarios where variables can go wrong and why.

Equals or not equals

'=' at the start of the variable, for example :

=sum(Amount)

The variable is calculated at the document level,

this does not take into account any dimension used in the table.

- this can result in incorrect calculations.

An example of this is:

1. Create a new document.

2. In the loadscript create an inline table using the following script:

   ```
   variable_test:
   LOAD * INLINE [
      Name, Amount
      UserA, 10
      UserB, 20
      UserC, 30
   ];
   ```

3. Create the following variables :

   user_total_no_equals:

   sum(Amount)

   user_total_with_equals)

   =sum(Amount)

4. Create a chart pivot table object with the following:

   Dimensions:Name

   Expressions:

   =sum(Amount) //user_total_with_equals

   sum(Amount) //user_total_no_equals

   $(user_total_no_equals)   //label No equals

   $(user_total_with_equals)   //label With equals

5. Your pivot table should look like the following screenshot:

Name	=sum(Amount)	sum(Amount)	No equals	With equals
UserA	10	10	10	60
UserB	20	20	20	60
UserC	30	30	30	60

60

Because the variable'*user_total_with_equals' starts with an = it* does not take into account the Name dimension when calculating the total of the Amount field.   You can see this in the column 'With equals' which has the total value for each row.

If you add totals you will see that they are correct:

Name	=sum(Amount)	sum(Amount)	No equals	With equals
Total	**60**	**60**	**60**	**60**
UserA	10	10	10	60
UserB	20	20	20	60
UserC	30	30	30	60

60

 If you go to the Expressions tab of the pivot table properties , selected the 'With equals' expressions and changed the total mode to 'Sum of Rows' , the total would be 180 which is obviously wrong.

Let or Set

The default is LET if you leave out the SET\LET statement.

For example add the following line to your loadscript and reload it:

my_test_var = today();

Check your variables in settings-variable overview and you will see the variable

my_test_var has been set to today's date.

SET

Set does not evaluated the expression after the '='.

At the start of the loadscript we set various variables to strings using the SET:

SET *TimeFormat*='hh:mm:ss';

LET

Let evaluates the expression before setting the variable.

For example: To evaluated a function and retrieve a date we use the Let statement.

LET *incremental_load_lastdate* = timestamp(Peek('incremental_load_table.created_dttm',-1),'DD/MM/YYYY HH:MM:SS');

Sql stored procedures

Update a sql server table from the loadscript

It is possible to update sql server tables using a stored procedure call when reloading your qlikview document.

Add a stored procedure to the sql server

ALTER PROCEDURE update_from_qv

@username varchar(100)

AS

BEGIN

      INSERT INTO dbo.users(name,created_dttm) VALUES(@username,'12/12/13')

      select * from users

END

In the loadscript add the connect statement and 'SQL EXECUTE' statement to call //the stored procedure

OLEDB CONNECT TO ...

SQL EXECUTE testdb.dbo.update_from_qv @username='me'

In this example we are passing the variable @username to the stored procedure.

6. Security – Section Access

QlikView Document security

IMPORTANT:

When creating examples to test security it is important to make backups of you QlikView documents just in case you get locked out of the document.

There are 3 levels of security that are normally applied in QlikView :

OS level security - if you are using Active Directory for the users to login to you qlikview server you can control whether or not a user can see a document in the accesspoint using NTFS security.

Server level security - See Appendix A.

Document level security - This chapter will cover qlikview document security.

Use document security for 3 reasons:

1. To prevent users accessing the qlikview document.

2. To filter the data within the qlikview document so users can only see data that is relevant to them.

3. To use other document level security settings.

By default if the user is given access to the qlikview accesspoint using Active Directory(NTFS Authorization) they will be able to open any document.

If there are documents that contain sensitive information one way you can prevent all users from accessing the document is by using Section Access.

Next we will describe how to setup basic section access and then how to extend section access to only display certain data based on the user login.

Finally we will cover how to change the section access script to access the section access data from outside the document, so it will be easier for non qlikview developers to update the security settings.

Section Access Security

The login using section access can be setup in 2 ways:

1. Setting the username\password in the section access script.

2. Using your active directory login which means that the user does not have to type in or remember another login.

Basic section access

In this example we will setup a basic section access script.

Two users will be added. 1 user will have administrator access to the document whereas the other user will only have user level access.

1. Create a new qlikview document and open the loadscript (File - Edit Script)

2. Add some data :

    ```
    important_data:
    LOAD * INLINE [
        USER, ADDRESS, ACCOUNT_CODE
        J. Bloggs, 1 Oxford Street, 123
        A.N. Other, 22 Some Avenue, 456
    ];
    ```

3. Create a table to display the data

4. Add the simple section access script before the script to load the table:

    ```
    Section Access;
    LOAD * INLINE [
        ACCESS, USERID, PASSWORD
        ADMIN, ADMIN, pass1
        USER, USER, pass2
    ];
    Section Application;
    ```

5. The ACCESS field is set to either ADMIN \ USER.

   Using other access levels such as NONE will be treated as no access.

6. Below are a list of protected field names, that have a special meaning in the section access table.

   ACCESS
   USERID
   PASSWORD
   SERIAL - QlikView serial number
   NTNAME - username\group name
   NTDOMAIN
   NTSID
   OMIT - list of fields to omit for this user.

7. If none of the security fields (NTNAME\USERID) are loaded all users will have admin rights.

8. Use for command line reloads of access-restricted documents.

9. All field names should be in UPPER CASE.

Your full loadscript should look like the code below:

```
SET ThousandSep=',';
SET DecimalSep='.';
SET MoneyThousandSep=',';
SET MoneyDecimalSep='.';
SET MoneyFormat='£#,##0.00;-£#,##0.00';
SET TimeFormat='hh:mm:ss';
SET DateFormat='DD/MM/YYYY';
SET TimestampFormat='DD/MM/YYYY hh:mm:ss[.fff]';
SET MonthNames='Jan;Feb;Mar;Apr;May;Jun;Jul;Aug;Sep;Oct;Nov;Dec';
SET DayNames='Mon;Tue;Wed;Thu;Fri;Sat;Sun';

Section Access;
LOAD * INLINE [
  ACCESS, USERID, PASSWORD
  ADMIN, ADMIN, pass1
  USER, USER, pass2
];
Section Application;
```

```
important_data:
 LOAD * INLINE [
   USER, ADDRESS, ACCOUNT_CODE
   J. Bloggs, 1 Oxford Street, 123
   A.N. Other, 22 Some Avenue, 456
];
```

10. Close and open the QlikView document. You will be presented with a a login box as shown, enter the userid of ADMIN and click OK , then enter the password of pass1.

11. Close and open the QlikView document.

12. If you are not presented with a login box you will need to either exit the qlikview application
    and reopen it or go to Settings -> User Preferences, General tab and make sure that the option 'Remember Login Credentials Until QlikView Exists' is unchecked.

13. You will be presented with a a login box as shown, enter the userid of USER
    and click OK , then enter the password of pass2.

14. When you login as the USER userid you will see the same data as the ADMIN userid.

Active Directory logins

To use active directory logins instead of a username\password you need to remove the USERID and PASSWORD columns from the Section access table and add a column name of NTNAME.

Section Access;
LOAD * INLINE [
ACCESS, USERID, PASSWORD, NTNAME
USER, *, *, MYDOMAIN\USER1
ADMIN, *, *, MYDOMAIN\ADMINISTRATOR

];

Section Application;

If you are running this on your own computer you can test the login using the format of : COMPUTERNAME\USERNAME.

I normally have a test user login created in the Active Directory so I can check security with a user who doesn't have any ADMIN level privileges.

1. To run the qlikview desktop application as a different user simply go to the C:\Program Files\QlikView folder , hold CTRL+SHIFT and right click on the Qv.exe file and select Run as a different user.

2. It is common to have a mixture of Active Directory logins and Userid\password logins.

3. In this case any field that is not used can be replaced with an * as show in the example below:

Section Access;
LOAD * INLINE [
ACCESS, USERID, PASSWORD, NTNAME
USER, *, *, MYDOMAIN\USER1
USER, *, *, MYDOMAIN\USER2

ADMIN, *, *, MYDOMAIN\ADMINISTRATOR

ADMIN,ADMIN,ADMIN,*
];
Section Application;

Filter the data within the qlikview document

Next we will extend the previous example to filter records based on the user login.

In this example the userid USER will only see 1 record whereas the ADMIN userid

will see all the records.

1. To filter the data when the document is loaded we need to add a column to the

section access table and create a section application table which will be used to

filter the data in the rest of the document.

2. In this example we are going to go back to the security example that does not

use active directory and add the column COUNTRY to the Section Access table.

```
Section Access;
LOAD * INLINE [
   ACCESS, USERID, PASSWORD,        COUNTRY
   ADMIN,  ADMIN,      pass1,       ALL

   USER, USER1, pass1,        US
   USER, USER2, pass2,        UK

   USER, USER3, pass3,        UK,US
];

important_data:
 LOAD * INLINE [
   USER, ADDRESS, ACCOUNT_CODE
   J. Bloggs, 1 Oxford Street, 123
   A.N. Other, 22 Some Avenue, 456

   DE User, 22 Some Avenue, 10

];
```

3. Next we need to add a Section Application table just below the Section Application table.

   The first column in this table is COUNTRY so it links to the Section Access, the second
   column is ACCOUNT_CODE which is used to link to the important_data table and filter
   the data.

Section Application;

```
STAR is *;
section_app:
LOAD * INLINE [
  COUNTRY, ACCOUNT_CODE
  ALL,  *
  UK , 123
];
```

4. If you reload the document and reopen it again and type in the userid USER and the pass2 password you will see that you still see all the records.

5. To reduce the records based on the section access\application open the Document Properties->Opening tab and check 'Initial Data Reduction Based on Section Access' option.

6. Strict Exclusion option - if not admin, the user is denied access if there are no matching fields in the section access.

```
Section Access;
LOAD * INLINE [
  ACCESS, USERID, PASSWORD,        COUNTRY
  ADMIN,  ADMIN,      pass1,       ALL
  USER, USER1, pass1,        ALL
  USER, USER2, pass2,        UK
  USER, USER3, pass3,        UK,US
];
```

Section Application;

```
STAR is *;
section_app:
LOAD * INLINE [
  COUNTRY, ACCOUNT_CODE
  ALL,  *
  UK,   123

  US,   10
];
```

```
important_data:
 LOAD * INLINE [
  USER, ADDRESS, ACCOUNT_CODE
```

```
        J. Bloggs, 1 Oxford Street,    123
        A.N. Other, 22 Some Avenue, 456
        DE User, 22 Some Avenue,    10
```

```
];
```

7. In this case USER1 will display all records but USER2 will only see the ACCOUNT_CODE 123 record.

8. The STAR is command represents the set of all values used in the table.

    If you comment out the line STAR is *, reload the document, login as USER1

    Section Application;

    ```
    //STAR is *;
    section_app:
    LOAD * INLINE [
      COUNTRY, ACCOUNT_CODE
      ALL,   *
      UK, 123
    ];
    ```

9. The following table will be displayed. This because the * in the ACCOUNT_CODE field is read as the asterix symbol rather than all the values of the ACCOUNT_CODE field used in the Section Application table.

USER	ADDRESS	ACCOUNT_CODE
-	-	*

Other document level security settings

To view the current document level security settings for the logins setup with an ACCESS level of USER in the Section access table to go the menu option:

Settings - Document properties – Security tab

Below are the default security settings:

User Privileges

☑	Reduce Data
☑	Add Sheets
☑	Edit Script
☑	Reload
☑	Partial Reload
☑	Edit Module
☑	Save Document (Users)
☑	Access Document Properties (Users)
☑	Promote/Demote Sheets
☑	Allow Export
☐	Allow Print (When Export Is Prohibited)
☑	Access Tabrow Properties
☐	Macro Override Security
☐	Show All Sheets and Objects
☐	Show Progress for Hidden Script
☑	Allow User Reload
☐	Admin Override Security

Admin override security – it is important to check this option so that the

ADMIN login in your section access has full access and is not restricted by the User privileges.

When you change the security settings you just need to save the document, close the document and then reopen it for the changes to take effect.

NOTE: The 'Allow User Reload' option overrides the Reload option when the document is opened by a user with user privileges.

Section Access Using Other Data Sources

Section Access From A Spreadsheet

You can simply replace the inline commands with a LOAD statement from a spreadsheet.

The advantage is that another user can update the security settings without having to open and update the qlikview document.

The only downside is that you still have to wait for the document to reload before any changes in the section access take effect.

```
Section Access;
LOAD ACCESS,
    USERID,
    PASSWORD
FROM
[excel_section_access.xls]
(biff, embedded labels, table is [section_access$]);

Section Application;
LOAD COUNTRY,
    ACCOUNT_CODE
FROM
[excel_section_access.xls]
(biff, embedded labels, table is [section_application$]);
```

Just as you can change the section access tables to be read from a spreadsheet you can also read the tables from a database connection just as you would read any other table of data.

Section Access Management In QMC

Next we will cover how you can use the QlikView Management Console(QMC) to setup section access tables. The QMC is only available if you have access to a QlikView Server.

1. Open the QMC , go to the Users tab, then Section Access Management.

2. Click the + icon in the right had corner to add a section access table ie: sec_test.

3. Click Apply.

4. Select the table in the left hand column.

5. You can click the Edit Columns button to change the columns uses for example if you are using the NTNAME or a USERID and PASSWORD combination.

6. In this example add the following columns:ACCESS, USERID, PASSWORD

7. Click OK.

8. Use the add row and copy row buttons to generate the table as shown.

9. Change the access level where required.

10. Click Apply.

11. Click on the Section Access Tables folder

12. Click on the Section Access Table Url:

    http://testserver:4780/QMS/AuthTable

13. If you right click on this webpage and select view source you will see that it is simply some html tables.

14. This is the URL to use in the section access.

15. Go to the loadscript.

16. Delete the current section access table so you just have:

    Section Access;

17. Position the cursor just below and click the web files button. Enter the url to the section access table (point 12) , click next and you should see a preview of the data that will be read from the html table. Click Finish and code similar to the script below will be added to your loadscript:

```
Section Access;
LOAD ACCESS,
    USERID,
    PASSWORD
FROM
[http://testserver:4780/QMS/AuthTable]
(html, codepage is 1252, embedded labels, table is sec_test);
```

18. As usual if you add a row to the security table you will need to reload the document before you can use the USERID.

19. If you have not used the web files button in the loadscript before you test it using html tables from the internet such as:

    http://en.wikipedia.org/wiki/List_of_countries_with_McDonald%27s_franchises

    or a more useful might be that of share prices from the following url:

    http://www.morningstar.co.uk/uk/equities/indexstockprices.aspx?index=FTSE_100

Hidden Scripts

Hidden scripts allow you to add an extra password to protect the section access and any other scripts within the loadscript.

To create:

1. From the loadscript select File -> Create Hidden Script.

2. Add a password that you are sure you will remember.

3. Hidden scripts are executed before the rest of the loadscript.

4. Hidden scripts are normally used to give extra security to section access code.

Binary Statement

Use the binary statement to load access and data of an existing qlikview document.

Only one binary statement allowed in your qlikview document.

Binary statement can load multiple tables whereas QVDs load only one table at a time.

1. From the loadscript select the QlikView file button and select the qvw file to use with the binary statement.

2. The following command will be entered at the top of the load script.

   Binary [c:\qlikview\binary test.qvw];

3. Because the Binary statement must be the first statement, if used it cannot be used with a hidden script.

4. For example:

IMPORTANT - Remember to make it the first statement in your LOAD script:

If the document is not distributed by the QlikView server then click Prohibit Binary load in the Settings->Document properties->Opening tab. The 'Prohibit Binary load' will provide extra security to your document by preventing anyone from loading your document into their own using the binary statement.

Conclusion – What Next ?

Now that you have completed this book you should have a better understanding of what qlikview has to offer when developing qlikview documents.

The examples in this book are just of the start of your learning in these more advanced topics as it is only when you start to apply techniques such as incremental loads for QVDs or creating your own custom data source connectors will you gain a clearer understanding of how useful these techniques are.

Some suggestions on tasks to cover next would be :

1. Creating a library of scripts that you can use to develop qlikview documents faster, for example loadscripts to perform set tasks such as reading data from multiple excel spreadsheets.

2. Practising creating different designs and layouts of the same qlikview document to see which you think work better. For example creating your own set of Themes.

3. Creating a data model with multiple fact tables.

4. At work it is work looking a the various qlikview log files to see how the qlikview server is being used and also the QMS API which can be used to perform various tasks such as managing document licenses.

Good luck in your future qlikview development.

Mark

Appendix A:QlikView Server - QlikView at Work

QlikView server is used to share your QlikView documents with other users.

Currently there is no trial version of the QlikView server available for download.

Therefore the first time that you will probably start using the QlikView server is when you are working within a company. If you do not have access to a QlikView server license this chapter can prove useful to prepare yourself for working on a Qlikview server and demonstrate that the installation and initial configuration of the server need not be a complex task.

This chapter will provide you with a guide to the installation and setup of the QlikView server as well as information on how you can write applications that work with the QlikView server and various QlikView Server security settings.

Below is a list of the topics that we will cover in this chapter:

1. QlikView Server overview

2. QlikView Server Installation

3. QlikView Management Console

4. Qlikview Accesspoint

5. QlikView Server Security

6. QlikView WebServer

7. Client Access Licenses

8. Reloading documents

9. QlikView and Visual Studio

10. QlikView Server Tools

11. Which QlikView Client

NOTE: the QlikView server installation in this chapter was performed using QlikView server version 11 SR2 and Microsoft Windows server 20 08 R2.

QlikView Server Overview

In this section we are going to provide a brief overview of the QlikView server.

There are several windows services that are part of the QlikView server, these are:

QlikView Management Service (QMS)
The QlikView management service is used to run the QlikView management console. It is the management console that configures the other services using the website running on the following URL:

http://yourserver:4780/qmc/default.htm

QlikView Distribution Service (QDS)
The QlikView distribution service is used to reload the QlikView documents based on some trigger such as a schedule or an event such as another QlikView document reloading.

QlikView Directory Service Connector (QDS)
The QlikView directory service connector is used to authenticate users. Various directories can be used to authenticate users most common ones are Microsoft Active directory or you can setup your own custom directory.

QlikView Server (QVS)
The QlikView server service, the main qlikview server service
This service runs a process called qvs.exe which will normally be the process that uses the most RAM on your server.

QlikView Webserver (QVWS)
The QlikView WebServer is provided as alternative to using Microsoft IIS.

The QlikView WebServer service is used to run this WebServer so that users can gain access to the QlikView documents using the accesspoint website on the following default URL:

http://yourserver/qlikview/index.htm

If you install QlikView server to work with the Microsoft IIS server there will be another service installed called 'QlikView settings service'.

The configuration files for each of these services can be found within the folder:

C:\ProgramData\QlikTech

(For Windows 2003 : Configuration files will be stored in c:\Documents and Settings\All

Users\Application Data\QlikTech)
 Within this folder you will find the following folders that contain configuration files for each of the QlikView services:

ManagementService
DistributionService
DirectoryServiceConnector
QlikViewServer
WebServer

The 'Documents' folder is the default location for your QlikView documents.

The lef.txt file contains the license information for your QlikView server. The lef.txt is a very useful file to backup in case you need to reinstall your QlikView server.

Also within the ManagementService folder there is a QVPR (QlikView Publisher Repository
) folder which contains configuration information for the management console.

It is useful to keep our regular backup of this folder.   It is also possible to configure the QVPR to save the settings to a database.

QlikView Server Installation

To complete this installation you will require a QlikView server license.

For this reason you will probably only carry out this installation if you need to use QlikView within a company as currently there is no free download of the QlikView Server.

Even if you do not already have access to a QlikView Server license hopefully by reading this chapter you will see that it is a straightforward process to setup qlikview so that other users within your company can access your QlikView documents.

In this chapter we are going to cover the installation of the QlikView server and its configuration.

1. Download the correct version of QlikView server for your Operating System from qlikview.com. Currently you can get version of the qlikview server for 32bit and 64bit versions of the windows operating system including a separate download for Windows Server 2012.

2. Run the QlikView server application, in the screenshot below you will see that this example is installing the 64bit version of QlikView server.

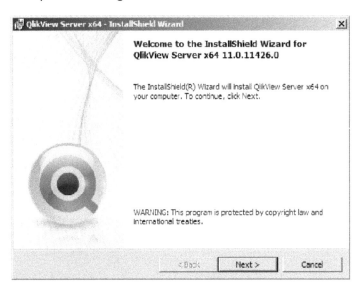

3. Click Next.

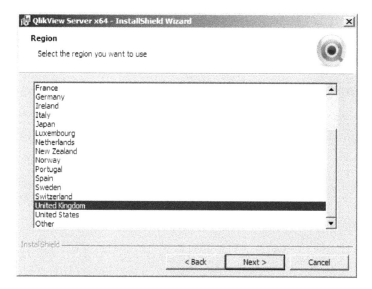

4. Select your region and click next.

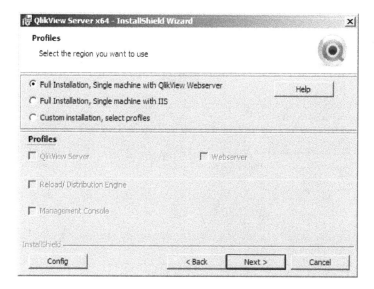

5. Select the profile to install, in this example we are installing the full installation which uses the QlikView webserver instead of using Microsoft IIS.

6. Click Next

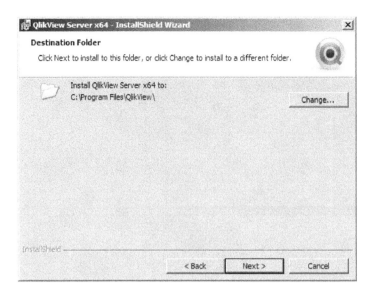

7. Select your destination folder for the installation, we have kept the default installation.

8. Click Next.

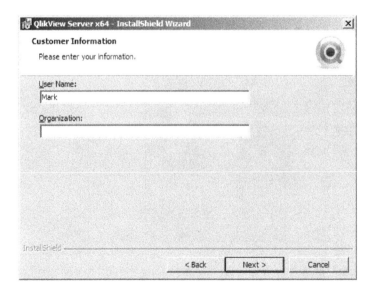

9. Enter your name and the company name and then click next.

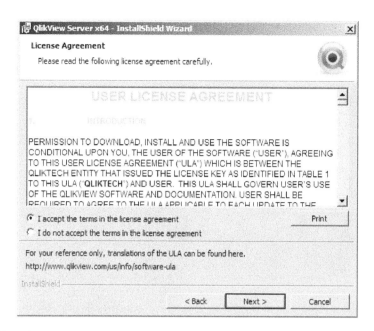

10. Select the option to accept the user license agreement and click next.

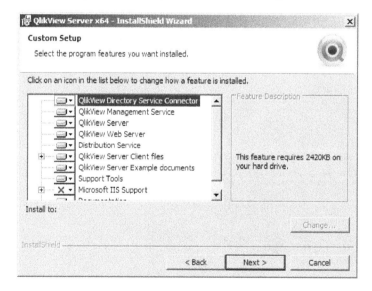

11. Click next to continue with the full installation.

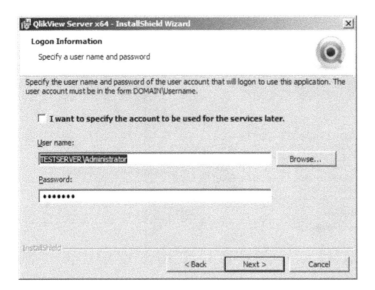

12. This account needs to be a member of the QlikView Administrators Group and needs to be able to access resources required by the qlikview server. Click Next.

13. Select the option to use the ' QlikView Administrators Group' and click next.

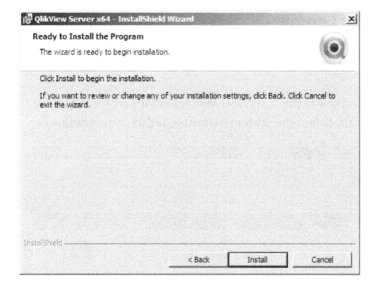

14. Click Install.

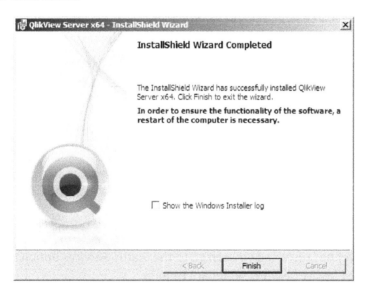

15. Click Finish and reboot your server after installation has completed.

16. Once the server has restarted you will see that you have 2 new programs installed as shown in the screenshot below.

QlikView Management Console

The QlikView Management Console (QMC) is where you will do most of the configuration for your qlikview server.

1. Click the Start button and select the ' QlikView Management Console' from the QlikView folder in the Program files. Select the System->Licenses tab as shown below:

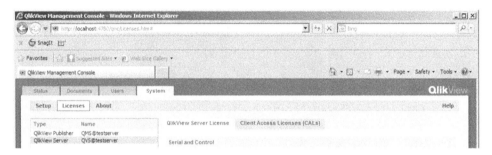

2. Select your QlikView server from the list of servers in the list on the left side of the screen and enter the details of your QlikView server license. Click the apply license button and a warning will appear informing you that the QlikView server will be restarted:

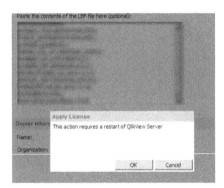

3. When the qlikview server has restarted you can go to the Status-Services option to check that all the services used by the qlikview server are running.

4. If you select the documents->user documents option you will see the example qlikview documents that are part of the server installation.

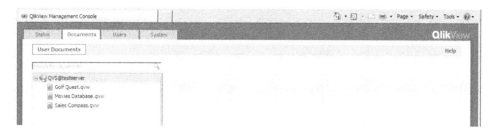

5. Select the system->setup tab and you will see the different parts of the qlikview server that you can configure including the qlikview server, qlikview web server, mail server and directory service connectors that are used for authentication.

6. Select the system->about tab to see details about the qlikview server installation and windows operating system. The client build number being the version of QlikView server that has been installed.

Qlikview Accesspoint

The QlikView Accesspoint is the website you will use to access your qlikview documents.

1. Click the Start button and select the ' QlikView Accesspoint ' from the QlikView folder in the Program files.

2. You will see the default qlikview documents that are part of the full installation of the qlikview server.

3. Click the 'Golf Quest' document to check the qlikview server is working.

4. If the document opens without error the installation of qlikview server was a success.

QlikView Server Security

In this section we will cover the different aspects of QlikView security from server Security setup to defining which users can access your server and what documents they can view.

We will start by covering how you can setup the QlikView server security to use the local usernames of the Windows server. We will also cover how to setup security to use the Windows active directory or custom directory configured on the QlikView server.

Setting up QlikView server security

1. To set up the security on your QlikView the server open the management console by going to the start button, then 'all programs' , QlikView and select the 'QlikView Management Console' option as shown in the screenshot below:

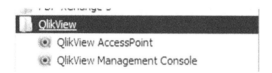

2. If you have problems opening the management console check that the account that is running the QlikView services has been added to the QlikView administrators group.

3. Once the management console has been open, go to the system tab and then select setup you will see options similar to the screenshot below:

4. The security of the QlikView server will be configured using options from the following three QlikView services shown in the previous screenshot:

QlikView Server

Directory Service Connectors

QlikView Web Servers

Next we will cover the options that need to be setup so that we can use the usernames of the local Windows server two authenticate QlikView access.

QlikView server

1. To configure the security settings of the QlikView server service select your QlikView server from within the system -> setup option of the management console.

2. Next select the security tab and you will see authentication and authorisation options as shown in the next screenshot:

3. The authentication options determine if anonymous access is allowed to the server.

4. Depending on the type of server licence you have you will have the option to allow anonymous access, for example , if you try to setup anonymous access when using a QlikView extranet license you will get the following error message:

   'Selected Authentication Level is denied by license.'

5. The authorisation options determine whether Windows security(NTFS) or QlikView (DMS) controls access. In this example we are going to leave the setting on the default option of using NTFS authorisation, doing so will mean that we can hide QlikView documents from users based on their Windows file security to the .qvw files.

6. For example, if we wanted to create documents that can only be seen in the AccessPoint by certain group such as managers we could:

   a. Create a Windows group for the managers.

   b. Create a folder containing all the QlikView documents for the managers.

   c. Setup Windows file security the folder that contains the QlikView documents for the managers.

d. Within the QlikView server setup, select the folders tab and add the path to the folder containing the managers QlikView documents (as shown below).

NOTE: The Browseable checkbox for each folder does not mean that the documents within the folder will not be shown in the Accesspoint but rather that the documents will be hidden when accessing the documents by other methods such as the File->Open In Server option from the QlikView desktop application.

QlikView Directory Service connectors

7. It is within the directory service connectors (DSC) options where you setup which directories will be used to authenticate users when they try to login.

Windows Active Directory and Local Directory

8. Most common setup for QlikView server that is used within a company is to use the active directory option.

9. To use your Microsoft Active Directory with QlikView simply:

   a. Select the Active Directory option then the directory service connectors.

   b. Click the add button on the right of the screen.

   c. Enter the path to your active directory, for example LDAP://mydomain.com. Where mydomain.com is the domain name of your active directory.

   d. Enter values in the username and password text boxes to specify the user that will access your active directory.

10. You can enter multiple active directories if required.

11. In this example we have configured the QlikView server to use the local directory as shown in the screenshot below:

Using the local directory is useful in scenarios where you have a limited number of users to maintain and no access to an active directory or other directory server.

Custom Directories

To set up QlikView to use a custom directory for authentication and authorisation you will need to make the following changes:

1. Within the QlikView server configuration change the authorisation setting to use DMS instead of NTFS.

2. Within the QlikView WebServer configuration change the authentication setting to use a custom user as shown in the screenshot below:

3. Select the custom directory option within the directory service connectors.

4. Click the green add button located on the right of the screen, then click the 'get default' button which is next to the path textbox.

5. Click the apply button at the bottom of the screen and a users tab will be displayed.

6. Click on the users tab and enter the username and password details for a test user such as those shown in the screenshot below:

7. Remember to select the enabled checkbox and then click the apply button.

8. Next, go to your accesspoint URL and test that you can login with the custom username and password.

9. If you are having problems it is worth restarting the QlikView services and check log files for error messages such as the directory service connector log files located in the following folder:

    C:\ProgramData\QlikTech\DirectoryServiceConnector\Log

10. You will notice that when you change the QlikView server to use DMS instead of NTFS that and authorization tab is added to the settings for each QlikView document (as shown in the next screenshot). Using the options within the authorisation tab you can specify which users have access to a particular document. By clicking on the pencil icon you can even restrict the time and days of the week the document is available.

Configurable ODBC

Configurable ODBC can be used to authenticate users and groups using tables within a database.

One scenario which you may use configurable ODBC is when the user has already logged into another website such as an extranet and the password has already been checked. In such cases you might use web ticketing to pass the username and list of groups to the QlikView server.

To set up configurable ODBC you need to perform the following tasks:

1. Create two tables in a database (this example is using sql server).

Entity Table

The entity table will contain details of the user and groups

The tsql to create the entity table:

```
CREATE TABLE [dbo].[entity](

        [entityid] [int] IDENTITY(1,1) NOT NULL,

        [name] [varchar](50) NULL,

        [descr] [varchar](50) NULL,

        [email] [varchar](200) NULL,

)
```

Both users and groups need to be setup in this table.
The name and descr fields can be the same.

Groups Table

The groups table is used to map the entityid of the group used in the entity table with the entityid's of the users.

The tsql to create the groups table:

```
CREATE TABLE [dbo].[groups](

        [id] [int] IDENTITY(1,1) NOT NULL,

        [groupid] [int] NULL,

        [memberid] [int] NULL
```

2. Change the authentication type on the QlikView WebServer to be NTLM.

3. Create an ODBC connection to the database that contains the entity and groups tables.

4. Create a directory service connector type configurable ODBC.

    a. Path = ODBC://sqlservername, enter a username and password to access the server and click apply. Click on the edit button.

    b. Change the following settings:

        i.   Conn db name: <db name where entity\group tables are>

        ii. Data Source Name :SQL Server Native Client 10.0

        iii. Directory Label: <label used when selecting different directories in QMC>

        iv. Entity Name : name

        v.   Entity table db name: entity

        vi. Groups table db name : groups

5. You can test the connection by searching for users to add licenses for in the qmc.

QlikView WebServer

The QlikView WebServer option is where you will configure the various settings such as authentication, logging, URL and ports for the QlikView WebServer (QVWS).
Below is a screenshot of the general tab. If you are using Microsoft IIS instead of the QlikView WebServer you will need to change the URL field to point to the website hosted by Microsoft IIS.

Below is a screenshot of the authentication tab.

This screen has already been shown in previous examples such as when using custom directories where you can select the type 'Custom User' or if using active directory you would select the type NTLM. Finally the type of header is selected when using HTTP headers to pass the username to QlikView for authentication.

When using the type 'Custom User' with a custom directory you are presented with a prefix field. The user does not have to use this prefix when logging into QlikView. But the prefix will be displayed when the user has successfully logged in to AccessPoint as shown below:

Welcome CUSTOM2\testuser1 | Favorites & Profile | Sign Out

If you do not require the prefix you can simply clear the prefix field, click the apply button and the prefix were no longer be displayed.

Client Access Licenses

Next we will briefly cover the different client licenses available on the QlikView server.

There are 4 different types of client licenses these are as follows:

Named user CAL

1. A named user can access as many QlikView documents as they like.

2. If you go to the system tab, select licenses, select the QlikView server from the list on the left hand side of the screen and then select the CALs tab you will see the screen as shown below.

3. To manage the list of names users click on the manage users icon which is positioned on the right hand side.

4. Then using managed users dialogue box you can add and remove assigned users depending on the limitations of your QlikView server license.

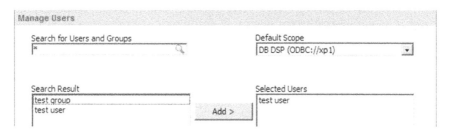

5. If you wish to reassign and named user CAL to another user you have to wait 24 hours while the license is placed in the state of quarantine.

Document CAL

The document CAL allows one user to access one QlikView document. The document CAL is assigned within the document settings in the QMC (QlikView Management Console). It has the same restrictions when transferring the license to another user, but has the advantage that it is cheaper than the name user CAL.

Session CAL

The session CAL allows the user to access any of the QlikView documents they are authorised to for a minimum session length of 15 min.

Usage CAL

The usage CAL allows the user to access any of the QlikView documents for a period of 60 minutes every 28 days.

If you have multiple types of CALs on you QlikView server it can be useful to know the order which these licenses are used. The New named\document cals in this list are ones that are being dynamically assigned. Below is the order in which licenses are assigned:

Assigned named user cal

Assigned document cal

New named user cal

New document cal

Session cal

Usage cal

Reloading documents

There are several ways in which you can reload the data in your QlikView document. In this section we are going to cover them.

Reload options

1. Within the management console select the documents tab, user documents , then select the document used to reload and click on the reload tab to see a screen as shown below:

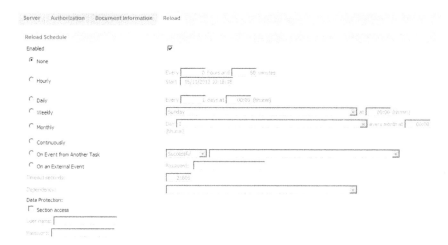

Scheduled reload

1. Within the reload tab select the hourly radio button, then click on the apply button.

2. You will see that the document icon has changed to show a clock which indicates that the schedule has been set up.

3. If you select the status tab and then tasks you will see that task has been set up for the reload of this document. From the tasks screen you can manage the reloading of the document as well as monitor when the document was last reloaded successfully.

One event from another task

Using this option you can trigger the reload of the current document based on whether or not the execution of another task was successful. For example, this might be used to reload the document when another task that was used to create QVD's completed successfully.

EDX - On an external event

1. This option will allow you to trigger reload of the document using a QlikView management service API call.

2. Select this option, enter a password and then select the status tab. You will see that the started\scheduled column now is set to 'on EDX'.

3. Go to the following url : http://community.qlikview.com/docs/DOC-2650

4. Download the following documents: QMSEDX_CommandLine_v1.exe (146.3 K)

5. Once you have downloaded the file and run the executable to extract the files.

6. You will need to alter the file that to point to your QlikView server.

7. Replace the text HOSTNAME in the following string within the QMSEDX.exe.config file with the name or IP address of your QlikView server.

    http://HOSTNAME:4799/QMS/Service

8. You can then create a batch file similar to the one below:

    QMSEDX -task="spending.qvw" -password=my_edx_password -
    qms="http://HOSTNAME:4799/QMS/Service" -verbosity=5

9. Replace the name of the task with the name of the QlikView document you have setup a password using the ' On an external event' option. If the document is contained within the folder you need to enter this has part of the task name as well in the format "it folder/taskname.qvw"

10. Once you have created your batch file you can execute it. You should see an output similar to the one below

    E:\QMSEDX_CommandLine>QMSEDX -task="spending.qvw" -password=markod -
    qms="http://192.168.0.12:4799/QMS/Service" -verbosity=5

    Successfully started task with id/name=spending.qvw

    Checking the status of task spending.qvw (id=2ae443f8-3269-4b87-bda1-31d3c3275ab

    9 execId=91f1c975-d8b1-4684-ba88-899be949c6e6)

    The task execution ended.

11. If you are familiar with Microsoft SQL Server Integration Services (SSIS) you will be able to use the execute process task to run this commandline tool and reload a document using EDX or your could use the Windows Task Scheduler to run the command from a batch file.

QlikView and Visual Studio

To reproduce this example you will require a QlikView Server license and a license for QlikView Workbench. If you are using QlikView within a company it may be possible to obtain a temporary license for QlikView workbench to assess these features.

In this section we are going to cover ways in which you can integrate QlikView documents into a .NET website using Microsoft Visual Studio and QlikView Workbench.

The first example will how you can build applications to query the management service and the second example will occur how you can plug QlikView sheet objects such as tables and charts into a website.

QMS API

Workbench

QlikView server normally requires an extra license to work with QlikView Workbench.

QlikView Workbench is included in the QlikView server extranet license.

To check if you are already licensed to use QlikView Workbench look for the following line in your QlikView server license:

WORKBENCH;YES;;

If you are licensed to use QlikView Workbench. You can carry out the following steps to start using it:

1. Make sure you have a copy of visual studio installed on your local machine. In this example I am using visual studio express.

2. Download the QlikView Workbench software from QlikView.com.

3. Install Workbench software. It is a simple install the only screen you need to make sure you get right is the one shown in the screenshot below, that asks for the URL for QlikView Workbench projects.

4. If everything is working you will see the message 'the requested URL was accepted 'when you click on the test URL button.

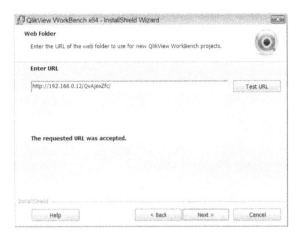

5. Once the installation has completed start visual studio and from the file menu select the new website option.

6. You will see that you now have the option of creating a QlikView Workbench website.

7. 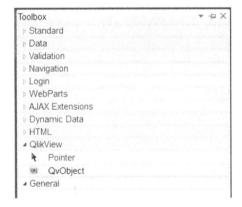 QlikView WorkBench   Visual C#

8. Enter the path for the location of the website and click the OK button to create it.

9. Open the toolbox and right click and select the option 'Add tab'. Give the new tab a name of 'QlikView'. Right click on the tab and select Choose Items. Click the browse button and navigate to the following folder:

   C:\Program Files\QlikView\WorkBench\Controls\QlikView

10. Select the following file and click the OK button:

    QlikViewWorkBench.dll

11. Options will be added to the QlikView tab as shown below:

```
Toolbox                          ▼ -⊏ ✕
 ▷ Standard
 ▷ Data
 ▷ Validation
 ▷ Navigation
 ▷ Login
 ▷ WebParts
 ▷ AJAX Extensions
 ▷ Dynamic Data
 ▷ HTML
 ⊿ QlikView
   ▶   Pointer
   ◉   QvObject
 ⊿ General
```

12. Drag-and-drop the QvObject item to your new webpage.

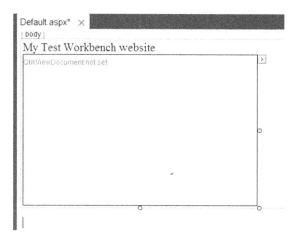

13. The following code will be added to the webpage:

    <qww:QvObject ID="QvObject1" runat="server" ObjectID="CH368"

ObjectType="Straight Table" QlikViewDocument="Sales Compass (QVS@testserver)"

14. Click the arrow on the top right corner of the QvObject item to display a menu .

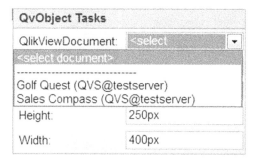

15. Select a document and object to display in your website and press Ctrl+F5 to run the website, and the qlikview object will displayed as shown in the example below:

Appendix B: QlikView Server Tools

There are some useful tools available for qlikview.

Next I will describe some of the ones that I use on a regular basis.

QlikView Powertools

http://community.qlikview.com/docs/DOC-3059

QlikView Server Super Agent

With the 'QlikView Server Super Agent' you can monitor multiple qlikview servers.

If there are any problems with the server you can be sent email notifications.

1. Using this service you add groups which are the server machine names.

2. Then right click on the new group and select add services to add the services

   that you wish to monitor.

3. If a service stops working the colour of the text and icon changes from green to red.

   You can also right click on the name of the server and laucn the 'Server Agent'

   which can be used to restart individual services.

4. The 'Server Agent' application is part of the power tools download and needs to be in the same folder as the 'QlikView Server Super Agent' if you wish to run the application from this application.

Qv User Manager 11

To use this with QlikView 11

1. Update the file qv-user-manager.exe.config to set the name of your qlikview server as show in the extract below you will need to replace the text YOUR_QLIKIVEW_SERVER with the name of your qlikview server:

            <endpoint address="http://**YOUR_QLIKIVEW_SERVER**:4799/QMS/Service"
              binding="basicHttpBinding"

              bindingConfiguration="BasicHttpBinding_IQMS" contract="QMSAPI.IQMS"

              name="BasicHttpBinding_IQMS"
              behaviorConfiguration="ServiceKeyEndpointBehavior" />

</client>

NOTE: If you have a non standard port settings for the QlikView Management Service this will need to also be changed from 4799.

2. Once this configuration change has been made you will be able to run commands

   such as the one below that will list the users that have access to this document:

   qv-user-manager -d="my_qlikview_doc.qvw" -l=CAL

3. This command removes all CALS that have not been used for more than 30 days.

   qv-user-manager.exe --remove cal

Appendix C: Useful Websites

These are some websites I recommend:

QlikView sites

- http://qlikview.com

- http://community.qlikview.com

  Obvious first source of information for QlikView and a great community of users.

- http://practical-qlikview.com

  The site for this book and other information about qlikview.

  Any corrections and downloads available that can be used with this book will be on this site.

Other sites ie: non-qlikview related

- http://Microsoft.com/sqlserver

- http://sqlservercentral.com

  Useful for all things sql server related.

- http://w3schools.com.

  For learning various programming languages such a javascript – this site is useful when developing extensions and macros as part of your qlikview development.
  Also the section on asp.net it useful for qvx development.

Useful Extension websites

- Javascript AP
  http://community.qlikview.com/docs/DOC-2639

- QlikView Properties Pages

  http://qlikcommunity.s3.amazonaws.com/misc/Qv11/qvpp.htm

- Extension Definition File

  http://qlikcommunity.s3.amazonaws.com/misc/Qv11/definition.htm

- QlikView Properties

  http://qlikcommunity.s3.amazonaws.com/misc/Qv11/qvproperties.htm

- QlikView JavaScript API Reference - Version 11

  http://community.qlikview.com/docs/DOC-2673

  http://qlikcommunity.s3.amazonaws.com/misc/index.html

Index